TOBAC̶C̶O̶ ̶S̶T̶O̶R̶I̶

From Myth to Mayhem

THE
TOBACCO STORY
From Myth to Mayhem

S.N. Chanda

BLOOMSBURY
NEW DELHI • LONDON • OXFORD • NEW YORK • SYDNEY

First published, 2017

BLOOMSBURY PUBLISHING INDIA PVT. LTD.
New Delhi   London   Oxford   New York   Sydney

ISBN: 978-93-86349-83-5

10 9 8 7 6 5 4 3 2 1

Published by Bloomsbury Publishing India Pvt. Ltd.
DDA Complex LSC, Building No. 4, 2nd Floor
Pocket 6 & 7, Sector C
Vasant Kunj, New Delhi 110070

Printed and bound in India

*In the
fond memory of
my late wife Ela*

Contents

The earliest image of a man smoking a pipe, from 'Tobaco' by Anthony Chute, 1595.

Preface

THE TOBACCO STORY is perhaps as old as the Earth itself. Since the pre-historic Pleistocene Era down to the ancient, medieval and modern times, it evoked awe and wonder, glorification, and ultimately condemned to the guillotine. From the time of primordial hungry man's chance discovery of the 'gift of God', debuting as a 'wonder weed' or 'holy herb', and introduced 'to the civilised man second only to food', and then crash landing as the 'killer plant', it is indeed an unparalleled saga. Despite stern warnings about 'nitrogenous organic element' contained in it, and nicotine's lethal effects on human body, people continue to 'smoke', 'chew', or 'sniff' tobacco, happily waving aside all caution.

Volumes have been written, supported by staggering data and poignant tales, and statutory warnings flashed across the world via electronic and print media, but all of it has fallen on deaf ears. As the saying goes: *all is fair in love and war*. The providential tobacco-human love affair shamelessly races ahead, past all hurdles, perhaps destined for a final date with the doomsday.

It is not my intention, in this small volume, to dig through the gluey mud of voluminous statistics about the once glorified and then much maligned tobacco habit. It is an humble endeavour to portray the age-old story of this enigmatic plant, in historical perspective, for the present generation, particularly the young ones, to understand, appreciate and assess the impact of this mystique weed on human body and mind, once considered to be a 'gift of God', a panacea for human sufferings or ailments, believed to be a source of solace to the lonesome soul and, eulogised by the literati and the intelligentsia.

S.N. Chanda

Introduction

AYAMONTE WAS AN obscure mediaeval town in south-western Spain. One fine morning the people of this sleepy township were aghast to see a man in the street 'releasing vile and noxious clouds from his nose and mouth'. The person was holding a crude lighted 'musket' between his lips, and was emitting smoke like a chimney. The townsfolk thought that the man must have lost his mind, or must be ill. It was indeed a shocking sight for the simple-minded citizens.

They discussed the abnormal behaviour of the man among themselves and decided to report the matter to the Inquisition, 'that most ruthless of crusades for religious orthodoxy'. The Inquisitors, as was their way, showed little mercy to the man. They stripped the man of all his material goods, confiscated his land, and threw him into jail for three years, or for seven years, the duration varying in some accounts.

The man was Rodrigo de Xerez (or Jerez), an able seaman and a trusted colleague of Christopher Columbus.

On 12 October 1492, when Columbus landed at San Salvador, one of the smallest of the Bahamas, now identified with Watling Island, he thought he had finally discovered the sea route to the Indies, and in particular to China. China was a dreamland in the European imagination of the fifteenth century, the land of 'vast wealth of gold, silver and precious stones, in silk and cotton, in spices, drugs and perfumes'. The indigenous people of the island of San Salvador regarded the strangers as 'divine visitors' and offered them fruits, wooden spares and certain dried leaves which emitted a 'distinct fragrance'. Columbus accepted the gifts. The fruits were eaten, but the 'dried leaves' were thrown away.

Certain now that he had arrived in China, Columbus dispatched two of his most trusted men, Luis de Torres, an Arabic scholar, and Rodrigo de Xerez, the seasoned sailor, to look for the Great Khan, 'the nation's ruler' and to tell him that 'Christopher Columbus, representative of a great people from very far away, would like an audience.' However, no 'Great Khan' was to be found. The emissaries of Columbus encountered only native people 'who were carrying glowing coal in their hands, as well as good-smelling herbs. They were dried plants, like small muskets made of paper…. They set one end on fire and inhaled and drank the smoke on the other….'

Rodrigo, in particular, was intrigued by the sight of the 'smoke drinking' natives and sneaked out a clump of 'dried leaves' into his baggage on his way back to the homeland. There in his home town of Ayamonte, addicted as he already was with the 'seeming enjoyment' or the 'spiritual bliss' of inhaling the smoke of 'dried leaves', he came out into the open with his 'offensive' display of public smoking. He was perhaps the first European to do so, his act landing him in jail for committing a public nuisance. By the time Xerez was released, smoking had already become a Spanish craze.

Soon after Columbus's rather accidental discovery of a new destination in the western hemisphere, the Atlantic waters witnessed a massive surge in venturing out to the unchartered shores of the 'New World' by plundering European explorers. In the fray were the Spanish, the Portuguese, the Dutch, the French and, a late-entrant, the English. These 'men of adventure', when they returned to their home ports 'carried with them as much of America as would fit into their ships, holds bulging with statues, trinkets, playthings, foodstuffs, objects of worship, articles of clothing, the old pieces of furniture, a few gold nuggets, a few pieces of jewellery, a few animals not native to Europe... And, of course, they returned with tobacco, the New World's biggest surprise, introducing it to the Old and wondering at what they had wrought.'

While most of 'old world' Europe had already had a tryst with the 'leaves' by early sixteenth century, it was not until halfway through the century that England had its first brush with this new found foliage. Sir John Hawkins (1532-1595), 'a stalwart sea captain and vicious slave trader', delivered the 'leaf' to his home land, England, for the first time as part of the booty looted from the tribal settlements along the coast of what we know today as Florida.

English seafarers and privateers Sir Francis Drake (1540-1596), better known as the 'Master Thief of the unknown world', and Sir Martin Frobisher (1535-1594), who made several voyages to the 'new world', were among others who forcibly seized tobacco, along with other spoils, from the colonial outback and native peoples, as well as from ships along the trade routes, and introduced it to England.

These adventurous English seafarers simply carried the 'stuff' to the shores of England, but credit must go to Sir Walter Raleigh (1552-1618), a 'dedicated social climber' and a debonair courtier, favourite of Queen Elizabeth, to make tobacco smoking a 'pleasurable' habit in England, by introducing 'something to civilised man second only to food'.

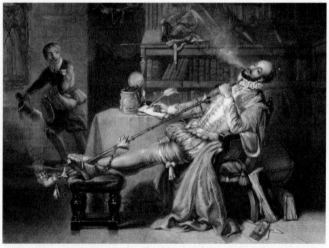

'Raleigh's First Pipe in England', included in Frederick William Fairholt's 'Tobacco: Its History and Associations'.

In 1584, the Queen granted a charter to Raleigh to 'plant' a colony in the 'New Land', an order he carried out and named the colony 'Virginia' after the Virgin Queen. Though the colony did not last long, Raleigh brought back with him bags full of shredded tobacco, as well as seeds of the tobacco plant for growing it on his estate in Ireland.

The story goes that Walter once showed up at the Queen's court with a pipe in his mouth. The Queen was intrigued and listened attentively to his raptures while he told her 'that tobacco gave him a feeling like no other he had known … it rid him of pain and sickness and would do the same for her in a matter of but a few puffs.' He further told the Queen that her courtiers and ministers and even some of the ladies were beginning to smoke and were much attached to it. He also emphasised that the Queen could trust him completely about this strange, foul-looking New World plant, and he knew so much about it that he could even weigh its smoke.

Elizabeth drew a bet for him to prove it. Walter thereupon called for scales. Pinching some tobacco shredding from the gilded leather pouch he always carried with him, he carefully weighed the amount he needed to fill his long-stemmed pipe, smoked it and weighed the ashes. Subtracting this second weight from the first, he produced the answer. An astonished Elizabeth paid him the wager remarking, there were 'men who turned gold into smoke, but Raleigh was the first to turn smoke into gold.'

The Queen was easily won over. So was the literati of Elizabethan England, men like Ben Jonson, Christopher Marlowe, John Fletcher, Francis Beaumont, and even William Shakespeare possibly. Suddenly, with the Queen's blessings, the puffed-up English nobility and the literati were found openly puffing on the 'foul-looking New World plant' in the streets of London, while London commoners were taken aback by the sight. The passers-by would often stop on the street when a smoker went by, staring at him as if he was an animal never seen in those parts. People felt agitated or angry, and were even frightened, at the bizarre spectacle that the smokers exhibited. They would often hurriedly run away, or at times confront the offender in a defiant manner, questioning his motives, or his sanity, or both. They would even threaten physical harm to the 'outlandish' smokers even though they could not muster enough courage to get close to the puffers in order to land a blow on them. Children ran away, hiding and casting disdainful glances at those men from a safe distance.

It is said, the first time Walter Raleigh's servant saw his master sitting on his favourite chair and contently producing smoke from his pipe, he was so terrified by the sight that he poured a 'keg of ale' over Raleigh's head. Despite the so-called 'keg of ale' story and 'scandalous behaviour' of public 'puffing' by a class of English society, the fashion gradually trickled down to the masses and roughly around the beginning of the seventeenth century, the 'pungent dried leaves' could be purchased at as many as 7,000 establishments in London alone.

It was, however, Jean Nicot (1530-1600), the French diplomat and scholar, who was credited with the greatest service in giving tobacco its official recognition. In 1559, Nicot was deputed on a special mission by the French Queen Catherin de Medici to Lisbon, Portugal. There he was introduced to the New World's 'biggest surprise', the tobacco, brought to him from Brazil by Luis de Gois, a Portuguese colonist in Sao Paulo. On his return to France in about 1560, he carried it (according to some accounts he carried snuff tobacco) as a precious gift to the Queen. The Queen immediately liked the 'sweet scented' stuff, and so did the titled personalities of the court. It was an instant hit with the nobility, the upper echelons of French society, who fondly called it 'Queen's Heat' and termed one of its preparations as the 'powder of the Queen'. From Nicot and the Queen were derived the term 'Nicotiana' and the protagonists of the Botanic Science anointed the exotic 'New World' plant, as *Nicotiana Tabacum* for the 'tall, annual broad-leafed plant', and *Nicotiana Rustica* for a 'shorter plant with fleshier leaves'. The nitrogenous organic property of the plant was called nicotine.

Part ONE

THE MYTH

The devil of tobacco 'drinking'. From William Hornby's
'The Scourge of Drunkennes', an anti-smoking pamphlet,
London, 1618.

The Oriental Connection

WHAT WAS REGARDED as the 'New World' by the post-Columbus Europeans was certainly not a new world. Traditionally known to the Natives inhabitants as 'Turtle Island', after the Iroquois Creation Myth of a handful of earth placed on the back of a turtle growing into a continent, the supposedly new world had been very much in existence since times immemorial. While Greco-Roman influence overshadowed the nascent European socio-political order, the western hemisphere witnessed the rise of unique civilisations. Olmec (1500 BCE – 400 BCE), Maya (300 BCE –900 AD), Toltec (tenth to twelfth century CE) and later on, Aztec Empires, blossomed here, oblivious to the European imagination.

But this 'mythical' landmass of primeval civilizations was not unfamiliar to the Eastern World. The navigators of the eastern world, particularly of the African and Indian mainland, were better equipped than the Europeans when it came to navigational knowledge. African seafarers were known to have sailed up to the heartland of the ancient Olmec civilisation. A recent discovery of a colossal Negroid head (made of asphalt), six to nine feet high and weighing up to forty tons, at the centre of Olmec Centre, La Venta, about eighteen miles inland from the Gulf of Mexico, is clear evidence of those archaic ventures of African seafarers. The African Bantu Islamic civilisation of the Swahili people was known to have been trading with India and China long before Columbus set out on his misdirected venture. In the thirteenth century, according to some accounts, a Swahili chief transhipped an elephant to the court of the Emperor of China as a gift. It was a historically established fact that there were longstanding and extensive Indo-Arab and Indo-Persian maritime trade relations since the first and second century BCE.

These primitive interactions between diverse civilisations resulted in the obvious exchange of cults and cultures, as well as transhipment of merchandise and victuals. One significant item thus exported out of the Eastern World to the people of the western hemisphere was a unique 'herb', by the African seafarers to the Antilles and to South America, as we know these places today. The Africans were introduced to this 'herb' by the Arabs, who called it 'tubbaq' or 'tumbak'. The Arabs in their turn were seemingly familiarised with this 'herb' through their longstanding maritime trade relations with India. Unfortunately, no historical account of such an interaction, is available. But, phonetics provides a clue to this (perhaps wild) inference.

Ayurveda, the ancient Indian medicinal repertoire, originating as an oral tradition in about 5000 BCE, mentions of a 'herb' as a remedy for phlegm, wind, cough, stomach wind, and as a laxative, cure for tooth ache, killing germs in teeth, banishing itching on the skin, etc. The recommended method of use of the 'herb' was smoking, chewing and inhaling. *Charak Samhita* (c. 100 BCE – 100 CE) and *Susruta Samhita* (c. fourth to fifth century CE), the reputed *materia medica* of the *Ayurveda* system of medicine, as well as ancient Sanskrit literature, refer to the 'herb' as '*tamrakuttah*', '*tamrapatrika*', or '*tamakhu*'. Arab adaptation of these Sanskrit terms as '*tubbaq*' or '*tumbak*' couldn't perhaps be ruled out. The Arabs introduced the 'herb' to the Africans whose enterprising seafarers transplanted the seeds to the Antilles and to South America. Tinos, the indigenous population of the Antilles adopted the new found plant as '*tabaca*', the nomenclature apparently coined by the African seamen, after the Arabian '*tubbaq*' or '*tumbak*'. When the Spaniards came into contact with the 'herb' or the 'dried leaves', they called it '*tabaco*', from which it can be rightly conjectured that the term 'tobacco' was derived.

One *Gentleman's Magazine (1788)* claimed that the term tobacco was a derivation of the ancient Hebrew saying: *Tob (bonus), Ach (fumus), A (ejus)*, meaning 'Good is the smoke thereof'. However, the basis of this inference could not be traced.

The Natives of Peru and Ecuador, of the erstwhile 'Turtle Island', were known to be cultivating tobacco between 5000 and 3000 BCE. By the time Christopher Columbus's arrived in 1492, it had reached every corner of the 'new world', including offshore islands, as well as Cuba. It was claimed that tobacco was 'as American as the Natives who presented it to the world'.

Some tobacco historians claimed that the western hemisphere was introduced to the tobacco plant about 18,000 or 16,000 years before Christ, when migrant Asiatic people first crossed the Bearing Strait and spread across the American landmass. At the other end of the globe, the Australian aboriginals, migrating from the South-Eastern Asian region about 40,000 years ago to that country, were known to be chewing the leaves of a kind of shrub called *'pituri'*, which has been identified as a wild variety of tobacco. In the backdrop of these revelations and the plausible Indo-Arab-African connotation of the term 'tobacco', the historians should, perhaps, attempt an in-depth study of the original habitat of the plant, for a possible oriental connection.

The Mystique Origin

I T WAS *TAMRAKUTTAH* or *tamakhu* in ancient Sanskrit. The olden day Arab world knew it as *tubbaq* or *tumbak*. The indigenous inhabitants of the 'Turtle Island' called it by a variety names, such as 'apooke', 'cohoba', or 'petun', and a mixed variety as 'kinnikinnick'. The Mayans and Aztec people called it '*iyetl*', '*piciete*', or '*pilico*', some of the variants as '*mai*', '*moi*', or '*mui*', and deified it as '*Anhel*', the rain and mountain deity, protector of mankind. But the origin of this phenomenal plant, what we know today as tobacco, still remained an untold story.

Palaeontologists at the Meyer-Honninger Palaeontology Museum, in Chiclayo, Peru, date the origin of tobacco to the 2.5 million years old Pleistocene Era, based on a recent discovery of small blocks of fossilised tobacco in the Maranon river base in north-eastern Peru. However, no evidence has yet been unsealed about how or when the first interaction took place between human beings and this blessed plant. Presumably, our primitive nomadic ancestors during their search for edible shrubs amidst wild vegetation of the primeval earth, adopted an 'eat and find out' approach and must have chanced upon a weed that curbed their hunger, cured some ailments, and incited hallucinogenic sensations in their body and mind. For our wonder struck primitive ancestors, this chance 'find' was like a 'gift' from the 'Great Spirit' to the human race. It takes us back to the imaginative insight of our ingenious primitive ancestors weaving incredible myths and legends or folktales, perhaps as a tribute or in adulation to the 'Great Spirit' for His precious 'gift'. Our quest for the origin of tobacco has led us to that domain of mystique, the magical land of these primitive narratives.

According to the Iroquois Creation Myth, Earth was a water-world in the Beginning, inhabited only by aquatic and airborne creatures. Up above, the Sky World was quite different. Human-type creatures lived there along with various types of plants and animals.

In the Sky World, there was a Tree of Life that was very special to its divine dwellers. One inquisitive Sky Woman persuaded her brother to uproot the tree to find out what was so divine about it. Beneath the Tree was a great hole. The woman peered into the hole from the edge and suddenly fell over. As she was falling, she grabbed at the edge of the hole and came away with some of the earth from the Sky World clutched in her hand. The airborne birds of the water-world below saw the woman falling from the Sky World and joined their bodies together to create a platform for her to fall on. To provide a permanent resting place for the Sky World woman, the birds and the aquatic creatures of the water-world decided to 'prepare the earth' by securing some 'earth' from the bottom of the ocean. Many of them dived down to the bottom of the ocean, but none were successful, except a muskrat which brought back a lump of 'mud' from the bottom of the ocean that was 'spread out' on the back of a turtle. This lump of 'mud' or 'earth' gradually grew into a huge landmass. The Sky Woman having found a permanent resting place on the earth gave birth to a daughter. The daughter grew fast and in due course was married to the 'West Wind'. Soon the daughter of the Sky Woman gave birth to twins. One was born the natural way, but it was a difficult birth for the other one, and in the process the mother of the twins died. The first born was called the Right-Handed twin and the second one, born the difficult way, was called the Left-Handed twin. When their mother died, their grandmother, the Sky Woman, in grief, took out the fistful of 'earth' that she had grasped from the edge of the hole in the Sky World, and placed it on her daughter's grave. This 'earth' carried a special seed from the Sky World. Nourished by this 'earth' over her daughter's body, the seed grew strawberry and sweet grass and a 'life giving plant', which the Iroquois called *Kionhekura*, the sacred tobacco.

A legend of the American Native Crow people recounts almost an identical tale, though with a little twist. In the Beginning there was no 'Earth'. There was only water all around. The only creatures were ducks and *Isa'kata'te*, an 'Old Man'. One day the 'old man' called all the ducks and said, 'My brothers, there is "earth" below us. It is not good for us to be alone.' He then instructed a red-headed mallard to dive into the water and bring up some mud. But the mallard failed in his mission. The 'old man' thereupon deputed a white duck, and then a blue-feathered duck for the job. But neither of them was successful. Finally, he entrusted the job to the 'hell-duck', who successfully emerged out of the water with a little mud in his webbed feet. The 'old man' was very happy. With the lump of mud in his hand, and accompanied by the triumphant 'hell-duck', he started travelling from the east, spreading the mud all around. Thus the 'Earth' was created. Travelling across the Plains thus created, he found a *bacoritsi'tse*, the 'medicine stone', which the 'old man' declared as the oldest part of the 'Earth', capable of reproducing itself. And that was how stones were found all over the 'Earth'. Finally the 'old man' noticed a 'human' like figure approaching him, and declared that it was an 'Earth-bound Star'. As the figure came closer, it turned into a plant, the first plant on 'earth'. That was a tobacco plant. The legend further states that this 'first plant' was a gift from the 'Creator' and it was incumbent upon every member of the Crow tribe to 'plant tobacco in spring each year with appropriate ceremonies, so that all needs of the people could be met.' It was because of this prophecy of the legendary 'old man', that it is believed that since ancient times, the Crow people have been planting and harvesting tobacco with religious fervour because they believed that when they 'stop doing that it would be the end of the Crow people'.

The Americas have had a long history of growing tobacco and various Native tribes have distinct tales to tell about this enigmatic foliage. The Huron woodland tribes of Central Ontario and the Susquehanna native Americans, inhabiting the area around Chesapeake Bay, believed that in ancient times, when the land was barren and the people were starving, the 'Great Spirit' sent forth a woman to save the humanity. As she travelled over the world, potatoes grew where her right hand touched the soil. The places where her left hand touched the soil, there grew corn. And when the world was rich and fertile, she sat down to rest. When she arose, there grew tobacco.

A different version of the divine woman's role in the origin of tobacco was prevalent among a section of the Natives of the Iroquoian stock. In the Beginning, the only means of subsistence was hunting wild animals for food. People starved if they failed to hunt. Once two hunters killed a wild deer and were broiling it, when they saw a young woman descend from the clouds. The young woman sat on a hillock and watched the men broiling the deer meat. One of the hunters said to the other, 'It must be a spirit, perhaps. She must have smelt our venison. Let us offer some of it to her.' They gave her the broiled tongue of the deer. The young woman liked the flavour of the broiled tongue and pleased as she was with the kind gesture of the hunters, said, 'Your kindness shall be rewarded. Come here thirteen moons hence, and you shall find it.' The hunters came back to the spot after thirteen moons and found maze growing all around; and kidney beans where her left hand had been; and where she had sat they found tobacco.

To the Algonquian Natives of America, tobacco was a sacred substance, 'originating from the bones of mythical First Mother.' In Pilaga mythology, associated with Argentina's Chaco tribe, Carancho, the Culture Hero, killed a cannibal woman and from her ashes grew the first tobacco plant. Mundurucu, the indigenous people of Brazil thought that the tobacco spirit, when still in human form, was buried under a tree and from his grave grew the first tobacco plant.

According to a Native American folktale, in the olden days there lived a man on the shores of a lake surrounded by large trees, deep in a forest in the region what we know today as Canada. He was a happy man with a loving wife and two beautiful little children. Suddenly, a cruel plague spread over the land and the man lost both his children and wife in quick succession. The broken-hearted man felt miserably lonely due to the sudden loss of his family. It was a long and dreary life for him and he often wished that he too had died. But he mustered courage and resolved to spent the rest of his life for the welfare of others and helping people in distress. Thus, the lonesome man found peace and regained happiness in life. He was held in high esteem by the villagers who affectionately called him 'grandfather'. However, as he grew old and was not strong enough to help others, despondency descended on him again, and he would sit alone for long hours on the bank of the lake, grieving over his long lost family and dreaming about his lost youth.

One day, when the grand old man was sitting by the lake engrossed in past memories, he suddenly noticed a large flock of strange-looking birds coming towards the lake from the distant Blue Hills. The flock of birds circled around the lake uttering strange cries. The people of the area had never before seen such large birds, or heard such strange cries, and apprehended some strange happenings. All of a sudden, one of the birds fluttered for an instant and fell slowly to the ground with an arrow stuck in its breast. No one knew who

had shot the arrow. The villagers were frightened by the sight
and gathered around the old man for counsel. Meanwhile,
the other birds screamed and circled around their wounded
mate for a while, and flew back to the Blue Hills. The old
man was not frightened by the sight. His innate evangelical
spirit was aroused and thought he must go to the bird and
try to heal its wound. As he was approaching the wounded
bird, a bright flame suddenly swept down from the sky to
the place where the bird was lying. There was a flash of fire
and the bird was completely burned up. Undeterred by the
sight, the old man came closer to the spot, stirred up the
ashes with his stick and found a large living coal of fire. As
he looked at the burning coal, in a twinkle it turned into
a strange figure like a little man, just about the size of his
thumb. 'Hello, Grandfather', the little man spoke out, 'do
not strike me because I have been sent to help you.'

'Who are you?' asked the old man. The tiny boy replied,
'I am one of the Little People from the distant Blue Hills. I
have been sent to you with a precious gift.' The old man had
often heard of the strange fairy people of the mountains and
was wondering what precious gift the Little Man might have
brought for him, but he said nothing. The little man from
the Blue Hills continued, 'You are old and lonely. You have
done many noble deeds by helping people in distress. In that
way, you have found peace. And because of your laudable
work, I have been sent to bring you more contentment.
Your work is done, but your life has not yet ended. You
still have a long time to dwell upon this earth. You must
live out your mortal course. You are always longing for your
dear wife and children, and you are always thinking of your

youth. Your days, as of now, are long and time hangs heavy on you. But I have been sent to you with a gift that will help you to pass your time more pleasantly.' Thereupon, the little man handed over a number of small seeds to the old man and said, 'Plant these seeds at once, here, in the ashes from which I have arisen.'

The old man did as he was told. At once, the seeds sprouted and long leaves grew from them. Soon, the place where the bird had been conflagrated became a large field of tobacco. The little man then gave him a pipe and said, 'Dry these leaves and place them in this pipe and smoke them. You will have great contentment. When you have nothing to do, it will help you to pass the time away, and when no one is with you it will be a companion. It will bring you many dreams of the future and of the past. And when the smoke curls upwards, it will bring for you many visions of those you loved. You will see their faces in the smoke as you sit alone in the twilight.' The little man said furthermore, 'Teach other old men how to use it, so that they too, may possess it and enjoy it.'

Thereafter, the little man abruptly disappeared, going towards the Blue Hills, never to be seen again in the village. With the fairy's gift of the tobacco and the pipe, the old man went back to his dreaming and found solace in life. That was how the story goes of tobacco coming into the lives of the Native American Indians in the olden days.

There are a few interesting and poignant folktales about the origin of tobacco from the Indian subcontinent. To the Baiga tribe of Central India, tobacco was more important than food or even liquor for living. These people traced this sentiment concerning tobacco to a time-honoured folktale, prevalent among this tribal community.

Long ago, there was a Raja whose only child was a daughter. Unfortunately, she was born with many physical deformities. She was dwarfish and cross-eyed. Her whole body was covered with sores and one of her arms was deformed. When the girl attained womanhood, her father, the Raja, went out in search of a suitable husband for her. He travelled many lands offering lots of wealth and property to the prospective groom. Many young men came forward, but they ran away at the very sight of the ugly and deformed maiden. The Raja tried his best to find a suitable mate for his daughter, but none came forward to marry her. The hapless girl was getting old. Distressed as she was with the situation, especially the pitiable plight of her dear father, one day she told her father, 'No one on earth would marry me. What life is this! Even animals and insects like ants, rats, birds, and cattle, live in pairs. I would rather die than live a miserable life without a mate.' Saying this she lay down and breathed her last.

The grief-stricken Raja copiously decorated the body of his dear daughter for burial. However, the well-wishers suggested that he should cremate it. Accordingly, the Raja prepared an imposing pyre and burnt his poor daughter's body. Soon, the body was completely burnt, except a small bit of the bone from her back. The soul of the girl travelled to the 'Great God', who asked her if she had any wish. The girl pleaded, 'I was very unhappy in my lifetime, as no one desired me. Now make me something that would make the whole world love me.' 'Let that be so', said the 'Great God', sending the soul of the girl back to the pyre and into the leftover bit of her unburned bone. In due course, out of that bone grew a lush green plant. And that was tobacco.

One day, a goatherd passed by on that way and noticed a lush green plant. Out of curiosity, he tore off a leaf and smelt it, noting its redolence. He picked some seeds from the plant sowed them in the courtyard of his home in the country. Soon his courtyard was filled with many plants. One day, he casually put a leaf of the plant in his mouth and chewed it, and found it to be extremely pleasant. Thereafter, he made it a habit to chew it every day. Once, he accidently discovered that if the leaf was burnt in a pipe, or rolled into a sort of tube, it tasted even better and emitted a fragrant smoke. The goatherd shared his pleasure with his friends. They took the seeds of the plant from the goatherd and sowed them in their own lands. That was how tobacco spread around the world. People immensely liked the taste of tobacco and its fragrant smoke, so much so that they would say there was 'no difference between tobacco and wife, we love them equally'.

The girl who had died after a lifetime of rejection, was finally happy to see that all the wise men loved her, and no one went to work without first touching their lips to the pipe, smoking in her fragrance.

Santal tribesmen, natives of eastern and south-eastern India, also recount a similar folk tale about an unhappy unmarried girl, who was unceremoniously cremated. The tribal god, Chandu, took mercy on her and said, 'Alas! I sent this woman into the world and she found favour with no one. I will confer a gift on her which will make men ask for her every day.' The tribal god decided to grow tobacco at the site of her cremation. In due course, the place turned into a lush green plantation of tobacco. A goatherd, during one of his daily chores, passed by that verdant green field of tobacco, and was surprised to see the goats of his herd greedily eating the leaves of the plant. Out of curiosity, he picked up a leaf and tasted it, but finding it bitter he spat it out. After some time, the goatherd boy experienced a severe tooth-ache, and having tried many remedies in vain he decided to try the bitter leaves again. He picked up a few leaves and chewed them, keeping the leaves in his mouth for some time. To his surprise, his tooth-ache was completely cured. From that time onward, he formed the habit of chewing tobacco leaves.

One day, the goatherd boy noticed a piece of limestone that looked like the bit of a burnt bone. He picked it up and rubbed it between his fingers. The piece turned into a white powder. He smeared the white powder in his hands and picked up a few tobacco leaves for chewing. Suddenly, he realised that the leaves tasted better. From that day onward, he started chewing tobacco mixed with lime, and the practice gradually spread among the Santal community. The boy always recommended the chewing of tobacco leaf to those who had a tooth-ache, or other gum ailments. Since then, the chewing of tobacco became a craze among the Santal tribesmen.

The Khasi tribesmen, of the north-eastern part of India, offer betel nut, betel leaf (*paan*), and a whiff of tobacco from the *hookah* or pipe to visiting guests or friends. It is a longstanding custom among the Khasis, as well as among many North-Eastern tribes, and also prevalent in other parts of India. There is a heart-rending folktale behind this sociable custom.

Long ago, in a Khasi village, there lived two boys, U Riwbha and U Baduk. U Riwbha was the son of very wealthy landlord, while U Badak was the son of a poor farmer. Despite huge differences in status, they were bosom friends, almost unseparable compatriots. As the boys grew up, they could not find enough time to spend with each other. U Riwbha had to look after his father's vast property, and U Baduk had to extend a helping hand to his aging father for tilling their rice field. But their friendship remained as firm as ever. In time, both the boys got married, U Riwbha to a beautiful damsel from a very wealthy family, and U Baduk married a girl from a poor farmer family in a distant village, and as per the Khasi custom, went away to the girl's village to live with them.

Circumstances kept the two friends apart, but their feelings for each other never abated. Whenever U Baduk visited his native village, he would make it a point to meet his childhood friend. In spite of his preoccupation with the considerable responsibilities of his vast realty, this friend would welcome his old friend and spend most of their time together. It marked the renewal of their intimacy and affection for each other. Once, when U Baduk returned from one such sojourn, his wife told him that their neighbours were making disparaging remarks about the intimacy between them and their wealthy friend. They believed that it was nothing but a false sense of pride to have a wealthy man as their friend. If the two were so close, why did only

U Baduk visit U Riwbha, and the latter had never visited him even once. U Baduk was immensely demoralised by these aspersions cast on his friend. When he visited his friend again, he asked him straight off, 'I am always coming to see you and partaking of your hospitality, but you have never come to see me once since I got married.' To this U Riwbha replied, 'Very true, my dear friend, very true. Even though my family business leaves me no time for leisure, I should have taken some time off to visit you and meet your charming wife. It was indeed my fault and I must make haste to remedy my fault. Give my greetings to your wife and tell her that tomorrow, I will pay my visit to both of you, and have the pleasure of tasting curry and rice cooked by your dear wife.'

A highly pleased U Baduk hastened back to his home to break the big news to his wife, and urged upon her to cook the most savoury meal she was capable of for his dear friend. Though elated by the news, a pall of gloom fell over her. She spoke out, 'It has come very suddenly, when I am not prepared. We neither have fish nor rice in the house.' A distraught U Baduk suggested to his wife, 'We have kind neighbours from whom we have never asked any favour. You must go out and borrow some rice and fish from them; otherwise it would be a great disgrace for us not to serve a meal to our friend.' The wife went out as requested by her husband, but although she walked the entire length of the village, there was no one who could spare her any rice or fish. She returned home empty-handed and informed her husband about her failed mission. U Baduk was extremely troubled by the predicament and wailed, 'What sort of world do we live in, where a morsel of food cannot be obtained to offer hospitality to a friend? It is better to die than to live.' Whereupon he seized a knife and stabbed himself to death. When the wife saw that her beloved husband was dead, she was overcome with inconsolable grief and cried out, 'What is there for me to live? It is better that I should also die.' She in her turn took the knife from her dead husband's hand and stabbed herself to death.

It so happened that that very night a notorious robber, called U Nongtuh, was wandering through the village in search of a suitable shelter to pass the cold night. He saw a fire was burning in U Baduk's home. It was dark and there was no sound of life inside. Presuming that the hard-working farmer family must be sound asleep, the robber sneaked into the house. Upon entering the house, he comfortably squatted down by the fireplace without being aware of the fact that there were two dead bodies on the floor. The warmth of the room made him drowsy and the robber fell asleep. Waking up early next morning, he was about to escape hastily when he was saw the two dead bodies lying in the room. Trembling with fear, he began to mutter wildly, 'What an unfortunate man I am to have entered this house! The neighbours will say that I killed these people. It would be useless for me to deny this, for I have such an evil reputation nobody will believe me. It is better for me to die by my own hand here than to be caught by villagers and be put to death like a murderer.' Hence, he too seized the knife and stabbed himself to death.

As morning advanced and noticing no sign of activities in the house of U Baduk, the neighbours flocked there to find out what the matter was. Seeing the dead bodies, they were filled with sadness and compunction, for they remembered how they had refused to lend them food the day before. Soon, U Riwbha arrived as per his promise, but when told by the neighbours about the terrible tragedy, he hurried into the room, sat down beside the bodies, and wailed loudly at the loss of his beloved friend. 'Alas!' he cried aloud, 'that a man should lose such a true friend because it is so hard for the poor that to entertain a friend is a greater burden than they could bear.' For many long hours, he kept on weeping, praying to the Almighty God to show a way of keeping up the custom of hospitality, without the poor having to suffer and be cursed.

During that time, the Great God was on a goodwill mission around the Universe and was deeply moved by U Riwbha's sorrow and wailing. The Great God instantly declared that from henceforth He would cause to grow three valuable plants, which were to be used by mankind in the future as a means of entertainment and hospitality, whereby the poor as well as the rich could entertain friends and relatives without being burdened. Immediately, three trees, which had never been seen or known to mankind before, sprang up from the ground where the three dead bodies were laid out. These plants were betel nut, betel leaf (*paan*), and tobacco. From that time onward, it became a matter of custom and etiquette in Khasi households, rich or poor alike, to offer betel nut, betel leaf (paan) and a whiff of tobacco form the *hookah* or pipe, to the visiting guests, or friends and relatives.

Another fascinating story about the origin of tobacco comes from the Arab World. The Prophet was taking a stroll in the country when he saw a serpent, stiff with cold, lying on the ground. He compassionately took it up and warmed it in his bosom. When the serpent had recovered, it said,

'Divine Prophet, listen, I am now going to bite thee.'

'Why pray?' inquired the Prophet.

'Because thy race persecutes mine and tries to stamp it out.'

'But does not thy race, too, make perpetual war against mine?' was the Prophet's rejoinder. 'How canst thou besides be so ungrateful, and so soon forget that I have saved thy life?'

'There is no such thing as gratitude upon this earth,' replied the serpent, 'and if I were now to spare thee, either thou or another of thy race would kill me. By Allah, I shall bite thee!'

'If thou hast sworn by Allah, I will not cause thee to break thy vow,' said the Prophet, holding his hand out to the serpent's mouth.

The serpent bit him, but he sucked the wound with his lips and spat the venom on the ground. On that very spot, there sprung up a plant which combined within itself the venom of the serpent and the compassion of the Prophet. Men called this plant tobacco.

Some of the tobacco historians believed that the tobacco plant, so extensively grown in America since time immemorial, 'was but a variety of an old European species'. The argument was chiefly based upon 'botanical, archaeological or linguistic grounds'. Discovery of a pipe in an ancient Grecian building in Constantinople that purported to have 'still retained the odour of nicotine', was perhaps one of the arguments to this conjecture. In the wake of this rather 'unorthodox' claim, and in our venture to trace the origin of tobacco, we came across an early Christian European story and a Flemish folktale, meriting reproduction here for the inquisitive readers.

God wanted to create the world. Thus, he ordered Lucifer (the Fallen Angel or Satan), 'Get me some earth from the depth of the sea.' Lucifer set off and after three days, he brought handful of earth and gave it to God. The curious archangel wanted to know what God was going to do with the earth, so he put some of it in his mouth. God scattered the earth all around and solemnly pronounced, 'Let there be a world.' The scattered earth began to grow, and continued growing for some time. God took a final look at the growing earth and said, 'it was all right.' Suddenly, He was startled by a loud howling and wailing noise. It was Lucifer in whose mouth the earth had also started growing rapidly. He was in terror and agony, and did not know what to do. Immediately, God ordered him to spit out the earth, and from this earth grew the tobacco plant.

The Flemish folktale offers an interesting anecdote. One day, a farmer, walking along a field, saw the Devil messing around with a new kind of crop, which he had never seen before. As a seasoned farmer, he was supposed to know every plant. Intrigued as he was, and even though he was frightened to come close to the Devil, the farmer asked the Devil what kind of crop he was growing. The mischievous Devil, with a treacherous smile on his face, said, 'So, you little farmer want to know what I am growing! Eh! Well! Listen to me. I give you three days to think and ponder about the crop. If you can find out the name of these plants, the whole field with all the plants will be yours. But if you fail, I will take out your soul.'

The farmer was seized with a keen desire to possess the land with the lush green crop of an uncommon variety. He accepted the Devil's bet. He thought, three days were long enough to find out the name of the plant, and gleefully headed back to his home. On the way, however, he suddenly trembled with fear and shock when he realised that if he failed to find out the answer, the Devil would certainly extract his soul. With a terrified look he returned home. The farmer's young and clever wife immediately sensed something was wrong with her man. When she heard the whole story from the farmer, his apparently unmoved wife said, 'Oh! Is that all? Don't worry. I will fix everything for you. Now cool down and have dinner and peacefully go to bed.' Even then, the worried farmer spent a restless night, wondering what miracle his dear wife might have in store. Next morning, the farmer's wife went about as usual with her daily chores. They had a quiet lunch together and then suddenly, to the amazement of the farmer, she took off all her clothes. She proceeded towards smearing a coal and tar residue all over her naked body. She also ripped open the feather-bed and began to roll over it until her body was covered with feathers from head to toe. She then headed for the field full of mysterious plant. There, standing in the middle of the field, she violently started digging it. Soon the air was filled with clouds of dust and the damaged plants were thrown helter-skelter. After a while, the Devil was on a round to check his plants and was appalled to see his crop being destroyed by a giant peculiar-looking bird. Infuriated, the Devil shouted, 'Damn! You cursed bird! Hell with you! Get out of my tobacco field!' So tobacco it was! And the bird swiftly disappeared.

On the morning of the third day, the wicked Devil was anxiously waiting for the farmer. He was convinced that the farmer wouldn't know the name of the plant. The joyous farmer soon arrived and told him that the name of the crop was 'tobacco'. The Devil was dumbfounded and left the place in a frightful huff, leaving behind a pungent smell and the 'tobacco' field for the farmer. The farmer and his wife carefully tended the crop and that was how the first tobacco-estate on earth came into being.

The Portable Altar

AN OGLALA LAKOTA hamlet was once struck by a tornado, uprooting trees, destroying houses, and killing men and animals on its devastating trail. People were running in a haphazard manner for safety. A lone *Unci*, the Grandmother, lived in a house at the fringe of the hamlet. A man rode by the house and said, 'A tornado is coming, and it is coming right this way! You better leave. It has already killed men and animals and destroyed houses.'

'No. I'll stay here!' said the Grandma. She then went inside the house and took out her little pipe, and prepared herself to face the storm. When she came out, the storm was already close by. The killer wind was blowing things around and a brown dust covered the air.

Grandma just pointed her pipe stem at the storm and prayed, 'Grandfathers above and in the four directions, please hear me. Grandfathers above, spare this house! I'm praying! Grandfathers!' Thus she prayed, and the storm split, passing by either side of the house and the grandma was safe.

It could have been a coincidence or a freak act of nature, but the Lakota people came to believe that it was Grandma's prayer with the pipe that saved her life.

Smoking of the sacred pipe constitutes an essential element in virtually all of the religious ceremonies performed by Native American Indians, from the north down to the south. Bowls of ceremonial pipes were often made of soft stone, from a quarry that they believed to be imbued with special powers. The pipe served as a portable altar for the offering of tobacco smoke, as a sacrifice to the Spirit World. Some scholars even termed it as 'the most ingenious religious artefact ever invented'.

About the origin of the pipe and its sanctity as a 'portable altar' there was a widely known Oglala Lakota legend.

Many many years ago, the Lakota people found themselves in dire distress. There was widespread famine and starvation. The tribesmen were fighting among themselves, and were in danger of extinction. One day, two desperate young men who had gone into a forest to hunt for food, noticed a figure at some distance. As the figure came closer, it looked like a white buffalo calf. The young hunters readied their bows, but suddenly the figure transformed into a beautiful woman. One of the hunters made an improper advance towards the woman. But as soon as he touched her, his flesh melted and his body turned into a skeleton. The other hunter, horrified by the fate of his companion, dropped to his knees before her in prayer. She identified herself as the White Buffalo Calf Woman, and told the young hunter that she would visit his people with a sacred bundle for the deliverance of his tribe. She commended him to return to his village and to tell his people to erect a big tepee, and an altar for her in the centre of the village.

The bewildered young man hurried back to his village, recounted the whole story to the village elders, and urged upon all the people of his tribe to prepare themselves to receive the mysterious Caff Woman. A tepee was built at the centre of the village, and on the appointed day, all the people gathered around the tepee in a circle, the elders positioned in the middle. From the heavens, an apparition of a white buffalo calf descended on a cloud. As it stepped on to the ground, it turned into the White Buffalo Calf Woman, carrying a sacred bundle.

After circling the altar, the Calf Woman opened her bundle at the centre of the tepee. It contained a *Chanupa*, the sacred pipe. She showed the people how to use the pipe, gripping the stem with her right hand and the bowl with her left. She filled the bowl with *Chanshasha*, the red willow-bark tobacco. She then walked round the tepee four times, in the manner of *Anpetu-we*, the great Sun, who circled around the earth. It was a circle without an end, the sacred loop, the road of life. Thereafter, she placed a dry buffalo chip on the fire, and lit the pipe with it. This was *peta-owihankeshni*, the fire without end, the flame to be passed on from generation to generation. The smoke rising from the bowl was *Tunkashila's* breath, the breath of the Grandfather Mystery.

She taught the elders how to use the sacred peace pipe to avoid bloodshed. The womenfolk were instructed in the right method to store and prepare food. Furthermore, she showed the people the right way to pray, the right words and gestures that they were to use. She taught them how to sing the pipe-filling song and how to lift the pipe on to the sky, towards the Grandfathers, and down towards Grandmother Earth, and then in the four directions of the Universe.

Finally, the Buffalo Calf woman said, 'With this holy pipe, you will walk like a living prayer, with your feet resting upon earth and the pipe-stem reaching the sky, your body forms a living bridge between the Sacred Beneath and the Sacred Above. *Wakan Tanka*, the Great Spirit, smiles upon us because now we are as one; earth, sky, all living things, the two-legged, four-legged, the winged ones, the trees, and the grass. The pipe holds them all together.' The mysterious Buffalo Calf Woman then disappeared.

Almost an identical tale, with slight variations in format, was also commonly known to the Oglala Sioux people. These tales, nevertheless, provided the necessary credentials to the indigenous people of America to pick up the habit of pipe smoking with religious fervour. It became such a fundamental part of their life that a man always carried a pipe and a tobacco pouch with him. Smoking pipe with the 'Great Spirit's' gift of tobacco was but praying. The smoke that was expelled was the emissary of one's prayers, an incense with a mission. People would blow tobacco smoke over their weapons and into the warrior's faces before battle, or use it as an insecticide for better harvests. They would blow it down the throats of the animals they slaughtered, as a protection from the creature's ghost, blow it over the dead bodies to honour the departed soul, and even on women before sex. The ceremonial pipe was taken around to recruit volunteers for war. Those who agreed to join the war, smoked the pipe to signify their willingness. Tobacco smoke was indeed a most venerable offering to the indigenous ceremonies for initiation, fertility or cleansing.

Knowledgably, three different kinds of pipes were used by the Natives American Indians. One that was of lesser significance was used by the people in general for social purposes, or for pleasure. The second was a personal pipe used for personal offerings, family bonding, for friendly relations between clans, or for initiating a truce with enemies. The third, the most important one, was the ceremonial pipe for sweat lodge rites, vision quests, purification rites, or for ceremonial dances.

Each ethnic group had its own conception about the size or shape of the pipe. The oldest known pipe was made of clay or soapstone, and sometimes had animal or spirit effigies carved on the bowls. With inconsequential exceptions, pipes were generally tabular in shape, and usually made of clay, soapstone, reed stems, wood, bamboo stems, animal or bird bones, and even ivory. The average size of the pipe was about six inches long and was made of 'hard wood scraped somewhat conclave in profile, the bowl lined with inset soapstone'. In some regions, six-feet long reed stem pipes were found with the end of the bowl abruptly thickened to two or three inches with a slender stem. The Cherokee Indian ceremonial pipe was made of stone and decorated with a fan of golden eagle feathers, dyed red and embellished with porcupine quills, woodpecker beaks and a tuft of red horse hair hanging down. The Oglala Sioux ceremonial pipe had four ribbons hanging from the stem, signifying the four quarters of the Universe. Most of the Plains Indian pipes were decorated with four or more ribbons dangling from the stem.

A typical example of an exquisitely carved Native American Indian ivory pipe (preserved and exhibited at Peabody Essex Museum, Salem, Massachusetts) was carved from a single walrus tusk, and elaborately decorated with pictorial carvings showing various animals and aspects of Arctic life.

Myths, legends, and folktales, unobtrusively uncovered the lid of primitive wisdom about the origin of tobacco and its sanctity, but the aura of those ethereal fantasies failed to throw any light about precisely when the human use of this apparently otherworldly plant began. About 5,000 thousand years ago, *Ayurveda* had recognised it as a medicinal herb. However, there are no extant chronicles of events or historical accounts to locate with exactitude, as to how or when the herb was put to human use.

The 'hedonistic' and medicinal use of tobacco were very likely to have begun through chewing. It was perhaps instinctive, as a corollary to the original 'eat and find out' experimentation, when our primitive ancestors found that the 'leaf increased salivation', as also 'pleasurably stirred his sense of taste'. When it was found that the leaf mixed with lime, pulverised shells, or other alkaloid substance, was useful as a dentifrice, as well as it curbed their hunger, produced 'a state of stupor' and sustainable energy. Thus our primitive ancestors 'readily fell into the habit of chewing' that gradually became a general practice.

Several American tribes were known to be snuffing or inhaling powered tobacco through their nose. How they acquired the habit remains a matter of conjecture. Perhaps, it was an intuitive innovation of the ever-inquisitive primeval mind. Snuffing of tobacco was a unique habit among some Native Americans. The snuff was prepared by drying and toasting the tobacco leaves, which were then pulverised. The resultant powder was blended and stored in calabashes or bottle gourds.

How smoking began has long been a subject of debate. It could have been an accidental discovery. Presumably, some wise man among the Native priests sniffed the fragrance of burning dried tobacco, and thus learned to combine pleasure along with his ministerial duties. Maybe, smoking initially was a priestly right among the Native Indians and the pipe, or a tube, functioned as an esoteric instrument.

According to some accounts, smoking among the Mongol tribes long anteceded the discovery of America. Based on the discovery of pipes (may be blowpipes according to some accounts) in ancient Greek, Roman, Turkish, Irish, English, and Danish ruins, archaeologists came to believe that smoking was an ancient practice in Europe as well. 'The Greco-Roman *materia medica* prescribed, on the advice of Hippocrates, Dioscorides, Pliny, and Galen, the inhalation of smoke for the treatment of asthma and some other ailments.' Later on in the middle ages, some noted physicians recommended smoking of various herbs for 'windy grieves of the breast'. The known source of the 'medicinal fume' was coltsfoot and even dried cow dung, but might not be tobacco as claimed by some archaeologists.

The earliest known portrayal of a smoker was found carved into the wall of the Mayan Temple of Cross, in the

Vase of the Smoking Monkey.
A ceramic artifact from the Maya lowlands created in
the late Classic period. A spider monkey possibly representing
a deity smokes a cigarette.

ancient Mexican village of Palenque, showing 'a pipe in the mouth of a priest, his head encircled by ornate patterns of smoke that drift around him and wend their way skyward.' The priest (or 'an impersonation of an aged God…with jaguar skin hanging from his shoulder') was smoking what appeared to be a tapering cigar with three bands that might have been a reed wrapping, symbolic of a tubular pipe. The ornate patterns of the smoke was apparently analogous to the blowing of smoke in the four directions of the world, as was the practice observed by the North American Indians.

Discovery of a foot-and-nine-inches long pottery pipe, possibly a ceremonial pipe used as an incense burner, found under the colonnade of the classical era Mayan ruins of the Temple of Warriors at Chichen (or Chinhen), Itza, Mexico, was an evidence indicative of tobacco's crucial role in the socio-religious ambience of daily life in the Mayan culture. The sacred Mayan almanac had portrayals of cigar-smoking gods of Rain, Death or Maize, similar to the carvings into the walls of the Temple of Cross.

Popol Vuh, the *K'iche'* (or *Quiche*), the Mayan sacred book of the Creation Myth, contains a tale of two heroes who were required to pass a night as part of the Ordeals they had to face in the Cave of Darkness, a haunt for the Spirits of the Underworld. The young heroes had to keep their smoking device, possibly a tubular pipe, alight all night to keep away the spirits of the underworld. However, they extinguished their pipes, and placed fireflies on the pipe ends to deceive their underworld antagonists. In the morning, they re-ignited their pipes and emerged triumphant out of the cave.

Yucatan Mayan candidates for chieftainship had to solve many riddles to achieve the desired position. The most ticklish among the riddles put to the candidates was to 'bring the firefly of the night. Its odour shall pass to the north and to the west'. The expected response was to get a smoking tube filled with tobacco. The riddle was designed to cross-check whether the candidate had sufficient esoteric knowledge necessary for his future office.

Tubular tobacco pipes were conspicuous as a divine instrument in practically all Mayan, and later on Aztec, essential rituals and ceremonies. These tubular tobacco pipes were known to be rolled out of raw or carbonised tobacco leaves, sometimes wrapped in corn husk, or leaves of the *nance* tree (*Malpighia glabra*), or leaves of *Guayaba* (guava) fruit tree (*Pisidium guajava*), or yellow leaves of an unidentified plant called *cocom*. When the Spaniards invaded the ancient Central American empires, and chanced upon those tubular tobacco pipes, they named it 'cigar', seemingly following the Mayan term '*sìkar*' for smoking. However, according to some tobacco historians, the term 'cigar' was derived from the Spanish word *cigarra (cigarro, cigarron')*, meaning the large balm-cricket, known as cicada, commonly identified with the locust. The body of that insect apparently resembled the roll of tobacco leaves in shape and colour.

The Vision Quest

AN OGLALA SIOUX priest once picked up a young man as a vision quester. Close to the fir tree forest, along the Black Hills of South Dakota, five wooden poles were planted in the ground. Beneath the central pole, *kinnikinnick,* a powerful mixture of tobacco, various grasses, bearberries, and shavings from the inner bark of trees, were placed. The young man was given a buffalo robe and a pipe. The bowl of the pipe was sealed with tallow so that it could not be smoked. The young man was left alone in the wood for what was known to the natives as the ancient ritual of *hanbleceya,* the crying for a vision, as a means to contact with *Wakan Tanka,* the Great Mystery.

Holding the pipe in both his hands, the young man initially roamed amidst the fir tree forest, and then around the poles, raising his pipe upwards in supplication to the sky and then to the ground. He begged assistance from the Earth, while crying out to the *Wakan Tanka,* 'to take pity on him that his people might live.' The penance had gone on for a few days, when the priest summoned the young man back to the fold and said:

'You have now sent a voice with your pipe to *Wakan Tanka*. That pipe is now very sacred for the whole world has seen it. Since you are about to put it in your mouth, you should tell us nothing but the truth. The pipe is now *Wakan* and knows all things, you cannot fool it.'

The priest then removed the tallow, filled the bowl of the pipe with *kinnikinnick*, and lighted it with a coal from the fire. After the pipe had been offered to the power of six directions of the Universe, and passed around the circle of listeners four times, the Quester began his report:

'Several eagles had flown near him, but said nothing. A red-breasted woodpecker, however, had alighted on one of the prayer poles, and he had heard the bird speaking faintly yet distinctly – "Be attentive and have no fear, but pay no attention to any bad things that may come and talk to you." Later on, he had seen the morning star change colour, from red to blue to yellow to white. Then just before the end of the vigil, the woodpecker returned and spoke clearly to him – "friend be attentive as you walk".' '

After the youth had completed his report, the priest passed him the pipe to smoke, and then summed up the lessons that could be drawn from the quest. The four colours of the morning star, he explained, represented the four stages of life – infancy, youth, adulthood, and old age – through which all creatures must pass in their journey from birth to death. The message from the woodpecker meant that the young man should always remember *Wakan Tanka*, as he walked the path of life, and remained attentive to the signs that the Great Mystery had vouchsafed to humankind. Only thus would he grow in wisdom.

That was indeed a unique primitive exposition on the philosophy of life, with tobacco pipe playing a vital role as a divine appliance for communion with the Great Mystery. The Natives of the erstwhile 'Turtle Island' spoke hundreds of different languages and thousands of dialects, or regional variations. Their cultural and religious diversity was enormous. Yet, tobacco universally played a distinct role among each ethnic group. Delaware Indians, during an approaching storm or thunder-gust, would offer tobacco to their 'god of air' to appease the storm. The Chippeways offered tobacco to the *Mannitto* (spirit power) of the water for a safe journey across the Lakes of Canada. Similarly, Mohawk Indians, when travelling across Lake George in upstate New York, would place specially prepared bundles of tobacco on a particular rock, believed to be the abode of their 'God of Wind'. According to a story, once when the Mohawk travellers were performing the tobacco offering ceremony in front of a rock, they were interrupted by a rude Dutch man, who scoffed at the whole affair, and turned up his derriere towards the rock. Consequences of his actions followed swiftly. The wind turned furious, capsizing his boat, and the Dutch man was drowned. Every Odawa Indian would start his day with an offering of tobacco each morning to seek the 'Right Path' and to cultivate a good relationship with *manidos*, the 'non-human power person who enliven the Odawa world'.

The Lakota holy medicine woman, *Wapiye' Win*, invoked the Spirits for ailing patients. An altar was prepared inside a closed room, surrounded by tobacco ties, that is tiny sacks of tobacco linked by a light string, and wooden staffs entwined with sacred flags at the corners, for each of the four winds. Spirit singers were called inside the room, and then the patient was instructed to enter through the door facing south. The medicine woman would hand over a pipe to the patient, forewarning that the 'Spirits will try to take it away from you. Don't let them'. Thereafter, sitting in the middle of her altar adorned with tobacco, called *Hocoka*, and with her head down, she would lose herself in a strange soliloquy, communicating with some invisible divinity. The singers would then blow out the lights and chant 'spirit songs'. Depending upon the ailment of the patient, the Holy Woman would then invoke the Spirits of Black-tail Deer, a White Owl, or an Eagle. If the Deer Spirit strolled around the room in a full circle, the patient would be cured. If it stopped in the middle, the patient was soon to die. The White Owl or Eagle spirits would come in with a rattling wind and the patient was asked to deeply breathe in that wind for a cure.

Tobacco in its various forms deeply permeated life in ancient Mayan and Aztec polity. The nobles, priests and commoners of these ancient civilizations considered tobacco as something like 'mysticism' personified, and adored it as an ally fighting beside man, to overcome fatigue or pain, or to ward off the human ailments of the body and mind. *Chacs*, the Mayan God of Rain and Lightning, was known to be a heavy smoker. When the God lighted his 'great cigar', thunder and lightning flashed in the sky and the comets were the glowing butt of the cigar He threw away. Tzotzil Mayans (indigenous inhabitants of Chiapas highlands in southern Mexico) considered tobacco as *Anhel*, the rain and mountain deity and protector of mankind. It was believed that *moi*, grounded tobacco, protected people from lightning and offered a cure for the harm caused by black magic. When rubbed on the forehead, and on the back of the neck and the elbow, it protected one from being seized by the dead.

The Lacandon Mayans observed 'cigar festival' to offer lighted cigars, made out of the first harvest of tobacco, to their gods, as well as to the village chieftains, to pledge allegiance to them as their overlords. Chorti Mayans of eastern Guatemala rubbed the saliva of tobacco they had chewed on the right leg in order to question the spirit *Sahurin*, who they believed, dwelt in the calf of the leg. The twitching of the muscles of the calf indicated an affirmative answer by the 'spirit'. No movement was taken as a negative reply. The Chorti Mayan medicine men also practiced a peculiar spitting treatment for curing and warding off the evil eye and 'strong blood', especially in children. The curer would chew tobacco leaves and spit his saliva all over the body of the patient, 'blowing or spraying it with a hissing sound through his teeth.' Indigenous Tlaxcalans of Mexico had an uncommon mechanism to ascertain 'god's grant of a request'. Large vases filled with finely ground tobacco were placed on the altars and benches of a temple, along with other offerings. Those tobacco filled vases were closely watched for a possible miracle to happen. After some time, the priest would examine the vases, and if tracks or footprints of some creature, particularly claw prints of eagles, were found on the ground tobacco, it was an occasion for great public rejoicing. This consecrated tobacco was considered to be highly efficacious against many ailments.

The efficacy of tobacco as a divine remedy for various types of ailments was evident among the tribes of both North and South America. Some would place plasters of chewing tobacco on the open wound to calm the pain. While others would rub tobacco juice into the cuts of men undergoing 'sacrification' (ritualistic austerities and/or self-torture like bleeding with cactus thorns or similar practices for initiation into religious order/sacred societies). Some would sniff powdered tobacco as a remedy for a headache or a common cold. As an analgesic, tobacco smoke was administered against toothache, and after the extraction of the tooth, a piece of the green tobacco leaf was placed in the cavity. For the pain of newly pierced ears, blowing of tobacco smoke was considered to be a sure relief. The blowing of tobacco smoke was also a general practice for bites inflicted by ants, snakes, spiders, mosquito, and other insects, as well as scorpion stings. According to a Tucano mythology, a dead child was brought back to life by blowing tobacco smoke. Even Tobacco enemas were known to be used by some tribes, both for medicinal and spiritual purposes. Tobacco was indeed a 'life giving' tool for the indigenous tribes of America, as it was believed to restore vitality to the sick and even, curiously enough, to the dead. It was an antidote against visible enemies, as well as invisible adversaries of the spirit world. Besides medicinal use, smoking of tobacco for 'social grace', or offering tobacco as a 'ceremonial gift' on occasions like nuptials or baptismal rites were very much a part of Mayan society.

The ancient Tarascan Empire (presently western Mexican state of Michoacan) rulers were known to have followed a unique technique before the declaration of war. The rival party chief would be initially invited for a feast, and the priest of the host ruler would burn a number of tobacco balls at midnight, a typical sanctification rite, by invoking the spirits of popular deities. Thereafter, two men would be deputed to place two sanctified balls of tobacco, two blood-stained arrows, and some eagle feathers in enemy territory, in the house of the enemy chief, in the enemy's city, or its chief temple. This was an act of witchcraft as well as a declaration of war.

The Aztecs worshipped Huitzilopochtli, their God of War and Hunting, and Ciuacoatl, the 'Snake Woman', patroness of war and goddess of pregnancy, childbirth and sweat bath, by burning tubes of tobacco in bundles. Proverbially, the torso of Goddess Ciuacoatl was made of tobacco plant. A tobacco gourd, filled with grounded tobacco, was the insignia of Aztec priests and medicine men and women, as it was among the various ancient tribes of North and South America.

Tobacco's association with the practice of Shamanism, the ancient form of priest-craft, was somewhat ethereal. Our simplistic old-world ancestors believed that the recurrent human conditions like sickness or ill-fortune were caused by supernatural forces, either by 'intrusion'—a form of possession, whereby an evil spirt or object enters the body of the sufferer, making him ill; or by 'soul loss'. Shamans, variously interpreted as prophet or priest, witch-doctor, spiritual healer, palm reader and even magician, served as an intermediary between men and the divine forces through 'vision quest' in an 'altered state of consciousness' or in a state of trance, enabling them to travel into the 'spirit world'. They could question the supernatural powers and/or the spirits of the departed shamans about the cause and remedy for human sufferings. In order to achieve this 'altered state of consciousness', the shamans subjected themselves to the rigours of 'psychotropic' and 'hallucinogenic' treatment, by using heavy dosages of narcotics of various kinds. Of all the hallucinogens, tobacco was considered to be exceptionally suitable as the sustaining agent to the shamans' transformation into a state of trance. Ingestion of heavy or repeated dosages of tobacco smoke or tobacco juice would produce initial nausea, heavy breathing, vomiting, and prostration (illness), tremors, convulsion, or seizure (agony), causing peripheral paralysis of the respiratory muscle, and thereby, the shaman would experience 'symbolic death' or the desired 'altered state of consciousness'. These 'tobacco Shamans',[1] as some learned scribes preferred to name them,

---

[1] The term 'shaman' originated from the Tungusic (the ethnic group of northern Siberia, Asian Russia/Mongolia) Evenki language, meaning 'priest'. Etymologically, it was inferred that the word was derived from Sanskrit *Sramana*, meaning a wandering monastic or a holy man. The Sanskrit word *Sramana* was said to have been inducted into various Central Asian languages with the spread and influence of Buddhism in those areas. Shamanism played a predominant role in almost all ancient and mediaeval cultures the world over, particularly in African and Asiatic countries, as also in 'pre-Christian Europe'. Tobacco shamanism was, however, a unique feature among both North and South American Natives.

were universally revered by the Natives of America as 'doctor-priests', who in their ultimate state of stupor would undertake 'vision quest', in the course of which they would supposedly identify the cause of the disease, and either eject the evil 'intruder', or retrieve the 'wandering soul'. It would thus lead to the sufferer's restoration to health. For their divine role, the shamans enjoyed a socially important position in their society.

Tobacco might have had its root in the Orient, or a possible link with some European species, or its origin may be dated back to the Pleistocene Era, but evidentially it was the Natives of the 'turtle island', present-day America, who had been extensively growing and using it in various ways since times immemorial. It penetrated deep into the socio-religious thought pattern of the Native American social order, and what apparently sounded as archaic or pagan, there was a profound beauty in those primordial beliefs and rustic customs or practices, inconceivable to the modern world. With the Spanish occupation of the ancient Central American empires, and later on, an aggressive colonisation drive in North America by the English and other European colonists, tobacco lost its sublime sheen, metamorphosing into marketable merchandise.

Part TWO

THE MAYHEM

A drunken party with men smoking, sleeping and falling to the floor.

The Brown Gold

THE RIVER *YEOKANTA*, as the Native Indians called it, originated from the Allegheny Mountains. Fed by numerous mountain springs, creeks, streams and swamps on its meandering course of three hundred and forty miles through the heart of what we know today as Virginia, spreads out into a five-mile wide water course before emptying into the Chesapeake Bay, and on to the Atlantic Ocean. The rich lands along the fertile waters of the river, with its verdant pastures and rolling farms, called *Tsenacomoco* by the Powathan Indians, was the home land for the tribes in Powathan's chiefdom – Appamattuck, Pamunkey, Mutaponi, Nansemond, Psape, Piankatank and other tribes, who had lived here since times long forgotten.

In 1525, the adventurous Spanish explorers sailed into the Chesapeake Bay and up the meandering river *Yeokanta*, looking for a shorter route to China and El Dorado, the fabled land of gold and silver. However, they had to turn back soon enough, abandoning their temporary settlement, as neither the elusive route to China, nor the land of gold were to be found (The Spaniards made an unsuccessful second attempt after about fifty years). The gold was eventually found in this river's 'quiet tidewater villages'. Ironically, instead of the proverbial glitter, its colour was brown, the Brown Gold, TOBACCO. However, another century would pass before the story of Brown Gold could be scripted, and the frenzied saga of a failed colony that dramatically changed the political chemistry of the world.

***

1494. Approximately two years after Columbus's landing on the shores of the 'New World', later on called America after the Italian sailor, Amerigo Vespucci (1451–1512), who discovered the source of the Amazon and circumnavigated the sea around the newfound landmass, Pope Alexander VI, a Spaniard, issued a decree for 'divided ownership of the globe between the Spanish and Portuguese.' There followed decades of hectic explorations and expansive colonisation. The world as we know today began to take shape in the sixteenth century, as places were discovered and named and new patterns of trade and cultural exchanges came into being. About the end of the sixteenth century, Spain, with the blessings of a Papal decree, and 'a blue-water navy no rival could match', turned out to be a military and commercial giant dominating over the two most important oceans in the western world: the Atlantic and the Mediterranean. In about a century of colonisation Spain occupied colonies, forts, and trade entrepots extending from Netherlands and Africa to the America, India and South China Sea.

That was the time when the sun never set on the Spanish empire. It was during that time that the Spanish sailors because of their interaction with the vanquished Mayan and Aztec people, picked up the habit of smoking tobacco. It became a 'strangely compelling' habit among the mariners and turned out to be a popular idiosyncrasy in the ports of Spain, Portugal, Holland, France, and even England. Along with their booty, the sailors returning from their transatlantic voyages carried back with them, the 'New world's biggest surprise', tobacco. The demand for tobacco was growing, but a returning mariner could only bring back a small and perishable supply – and there was no tobacco to be found in all of Europe. One day, someone would see a lucrative opportunity to make a profit in this. But the time was not yet ripe for tobacco to become a profitable article of commerce.

André Thevet, a Franciscan monk and author of *Cosmographie* (1575), upon returning from a trip to Brazil in 1556, brought seeds of tobacco to France, which he sowed in his garden at Angouleme. Even though Thevet was the first person to carry tobacco seeds to France, the honour was bestowed upon Jean Nicot, the French diplomat, who during his return from an ambassadorial stint in Lisbon, Portugal, in 1560, carried back with him some tobacco seeds and plants, which he presented to Queen Catherine de Medici. Tobacco was officially brought to Spain around 1558–1559, by Francisco Hernandez, physician to Phillip II of Spain, who was deputed by the King to collect specimens of flora from Mexico.

The initial introduction of tobacco into France and Spain was restricted to a limited cultivation in the gardens of botanists, herbalists and collectors of plant curios. Later on, when tobacco's importance as a money crop became apparent, attempts were made to grow tobacco commercially in various parts of France, Belgium, Germany, Holland, Italy, Norway and elsewhere in Europe. But tobacco grown by European farmers failed to produce a leaf that could appeal to the smoker's palate.

In England, it was then the Elizabethan Era. Adventurous and daring English sea-farers, Sir John Hawkins and Sir Francis Drake, who considered piracy as an act of valour rather than colonisation, were the initial carriers of tobacco on to the shores of England. In 1562, Hawkins was on a piratical voyage around the Caribbean, when he witnessed the 'Floridian Indians smoking'. Hawkins and his men seemed to have picked up the habit from them.

Francis Drake, on his mission to circumnavigate the globe, between 1577 and 1580, had encountered the 'weed' when he anchored on the Pacific coast of America near what we know today as San Francisco. The natives of the place, Drake recorded, '…were not only friendly, but subservient: when they came onto us, they greatly wondered at the things we brought…whereupon they supposed us to be gods.' The native offered Drake 'presents suitable for gods…feathers and bags of tobacco'. Drake accepted the gifts in the name of Queen Elizabeth and named the place 'California *Nova Albion*'. With bags full of tobacco on board, an elated Drake sailed back home to England.

Between 1580–1590, Spain developed many new tobacco plantations in the West Indies, as well as in their other American colonies. These Spanish plantations became the primary source of supply for duly processed and a milder variety of tobacco for the European customers, and Cadiz, Lisbon and London, turned out to be eminent ports of entry in Europe for the Spanish product. The 'strangely compelling' habit of smoking gained notoriety not only among the seamen, but also was catching up among the civilian population of Europe.

1584. Meanwhile, in England, something of an immense historical significance was happening. Reverend Hakluyt, an Anglican priest, an Oxford scholar and a visionary geographer, who spoke at least seven languages, was at that time serving as Chaplain to Her Majesty's embassy in France, the Queen's most sensitive post. In Paris, he was clandestinely meeting fishermen, pirates, mapmakers, botanists, astronomers, shipwrights, merchants, compass designers, furriers, sea captains, and anyone else remotely familiar with the Atlantic and the unchartered worlds beyond. The learned Reverend, who had never actually seen the New World, nor even travelled beyond London to Paris, with the information collected from various sources, worked out a case for England's participation 'into the New World colonisation game' in a twenty-one-chapter, twenty-six-word titled treaties, popularly referred to by the historians as 'A Discourse of Western Planting', which he hand-delivered to the Queen late in the summer of 1584.

Nullifying the century-old Papal decree about exclusive exploration rights to Spain and Portugal, Hakluyt argued that the Queen 'was fully entitled to colonise America', pointing to the legend of the Welsh Prince Madoc ap Owen Guyneth's exploration of North America in 1170, three centuries before Christopher Columbus had set his foot upon the New World. Elizabethan England was then a land with a high level of unemployed 'loiterers and idle vagabonds', bent upon 'pilfering and thieving and other lewdness'. Hakluyt argued that 'these petty thieves' could be resettled and put to work in America, 'enriching the Kingdom by mining the rich vines of silver and gold that undoubtedly awaited them; harvesting the primal forests for ship masts, pitch, tar, rosin, and soap ash; gathering hemps for cordage, honey for cakes, and beeswax for candles; dragging the broad coastal waters for pearls; cutting and shaping marble and other stones; tending silk worms, producing salt; killing whales for their oil, seals for their fur; catching salmon and herring; or raising cotton, oranges, lemons and figs.' Hakluyt indeed carved out a rosy canvas of opportunities for the 'rusting youth' of England as well as a charter for economic rejuvenation for the Kingdom.

Hakluyt's 'Discourse' must have stirred the ego of the Protestant Queen Elizabeth, who had been previously excommunicated by the Vatican on the ground that 'she was the bastard child of an illegitimate marriage and had no lawful claim to the English throne.' It was not known how precisely the Queen responded to Hakluyt's treaties, but she did grant a royal mandate to Walter Raleigh, 'her most trusted adviser' and a seasoned maritime adventurer, to set up England's first New World colony. Walter Raleigh was knighted by the Queen just few months before the historic mandate was announced.

The crafty Raleigh, landing on the east coast of the new world, above the then Spanish Florida, named it 'Virginia' in honour of the virgin queen. He 'deposited' one hundred and seven men (it was not known if any 'petty thieves' were included among them) on the shores of Roanoke Island,

and set out to the sea again, capturing the Spanish galleon, the *Santa Maria*, on his way back home. Those unfortunate settlers were virtually left in the lurch in an unknown terrain. When Francis Drake dropped by Roanoke Island two years later, only a handful of them were found alive. Those who survived begged Drake to take them home. A second attempt was made by Raleigh in 1587, to set up a colony at the same Roanoke Island by offloading 144 men, women and children. One John White was designated as the Governor of the colony. Soon the settlers realised that they needed more resources from the home land to survive. Unfortunately, the relief ship was diverted to fight the Spanish Armada. When the relief mission finally arrived in 1590, the second Roanoke colony had vanished without any trace. The fate of the so-called colonists remains a mystery till date.

Sir Walter Raleigh's venture to set up a colony in Virginia failed, but he was successful enough in acquiring an addiction to tobacco, picking up from the North American Native cult of smoking pipe and introducing it to his home land as a 'pleasure' habit, as recounted in an earlier chapter. Some of the English colonists returning from the failed settlement of 'Virginia', initiated commercial farming of tobacco in Gloucestershire and other places (1586). Despite best efforts, the resulting tobacco was 'poor and weak and of a biting taste'. The English neo-connoisseurs of smoking had to depend on their archrival Spain for their regular supply of tobacco, much of the stuff though was smuggled into English ports by the high-sea pirates, aggravating its already spiralling market rate. By early seventeenth century, tobacco kiosks sprang up on almost every nook and corner of London, even though its cost was as high as four pounds and ten shillings per pound of tobacco, while 'a mug of ale cost a penny and a young whore with good teeth was less than a shilling to throw'.

1603. Queen Elizabeth died. James I ascended the throne of England. Immediately thereafter, the new king, a hater of 'unholy' stink, came out with the *Counterblaste to Tobacco* (1604) and raised the taxes on tobacco by 4,000 per cent, both on imported (particularly Spanish), as well as on home-grown products. Meanwhile, Walter Raleigh fell from royal grace. He was stripped off of all his honours and rewards and was finally, by the order of the King, beheaded, at the age of sixty-six, in 1618, charged of an alleged conspiracy to dethrone the King. It was indeed an ignominious end of a rather over-ambitious and flamboyant confidant of Queen Elizabeth.

Despite Raleigh's failed attempts to 'plant' a colony in Virginia, Whitehall was abuzz with Reverend Hakluyt's vision of English colony in the 'New World'. Hakluyt's eloquent advocacy of the commercial prospects in the 'new world' was also catching up among London speculators. In April 1606, King James granted a royal charter 'to explore and settle Virginia'. The enthusiastic speculators set up a Joint Stock Company, called Virginia Company of London to fund and direct the colony. Hakluyt, who was by then knighted by the King, was one of the initial shareholders of the Virginia Company. In May 1607, three wooden ships – *The Susan Constant, The Godspeed* and *The Discovery*, set sail for the New World, across the Atlantic. The Company instructed the settlers to set up a colony, at least a hundred miles upstream of a major river, as a safeguard against Spanish as well as Native attacks, and at a place that could 'lead quickest to China, perhaps India'. Accordingly, the English fleet of ships sailing up the ancient river *Yeokanta* anchored and off-loaded on to a low-lying neck of a vacant land between the north bank of the river and a narrow, winding creek. The sailors named the ancient river after their King as James River and built a fort which they initially called James Fort, later on Jamestown, the first permanent English settlement in the 'New World'.

The Virginia Company had chosen seven names, which would constitute the Colonial Council. On the top of the list were: Newport, Gosnold and Ratcliffe, commanders of the vessels, *Susan Constant, Godspeed* and *Discovery* respectively; followed by Wingfield, a high-minded nobleman, John Martin, a seasoned sea captain, George Kendall, a representative of the Secretary of State to King James, and lastly, John Smith, a self-styled 'war fighter' and a daredevil adventurer. Regarding the duties and responsibilities of the colonists in the 'new land', the Company guideline was: 'once ensconced, the colonists were to be divided into three groups—one to build a fortified village, a second to plant crops and provide security, and a third to travel with Newport and Gosnold in search of silver and gold "carrying half a dozen pickaxes" for exploratory mining.' The guideline also cautioned the colonists to handle the Native Americans with 'diplomacy' and suggested bartering of copper and beads for corn and food, to avoid the danger of famine.

The first three years, however, were 'starving time' for the new found English colony. Shortages of food, aggravated by a prolonged period of drought, and intermittent unprovoked attacks by the Native Indians, despite best gestures of 'diplomacy' towards them, stalked the colonists. Deaths, due to near famine condition and disease, and by Native ambush, had almost become a regular feature. Moreover, the morale of the colonists was at a low ebb, as neither the short-cut route to China nor India was traceable. Also, they had not managed to discover the illusory land of gold. John Smith, the self-styled 'war fighter', who once ventured deep into the Powhatan chiefdom in search of gold, narrowly escaped beheading through a last minute surprise intervention of Pocahontas, the charming teenage daughter of the Powhatan chief. The much hyped 'land of opportunity and hope' turned out to be a pipe dream.

In 1608, Christopher Newport ferried twice across the Atlantic, with reinforcements of supplies and men, but the disillusioned colonists were desperate to abandon the fatal settlement. To vitalise the new found American colony, in May 1609, the Virginia Company of London 'shredded its old charter' and created a new post of governor under the direct control of the Company. Sir Thomas Gates was named as the new governor, under whose leadership in early June, a fleet of nine ships carrying about five hundreds settlers and fresh supplies left England for Jamestown. As bad luck would have it, it was the season of hurricanes in the south Atlantic, and in late July, the group was separated by a furious storm. After four days and nights of terror, the *Sea Venture,* carrying the new governor Gates and one hundred and fifty men, women and children, ran aground off the coast of Bermuda, miraculously making it to safety ashore. With Gates and his party presumed lost at sea, the rest of the storm-ravaged fleet limped into Jamestown in mid-August, carrying some three hundred men, women and children. They informed the colonists about the new charter instilling a new hope for the demoralised survivors. But with more settlers landing in the cursed colony, the situation rather aggravated for the worse. Scarcity of food and 'a bitter business of brutality and bloodshed' continued to stalk the settlers. A world of miseries ensued. Famine and disease took their daily toll.

Meanwhile, the Bermuda castaways, under the guidance of Gates, built two ships, from local cedar and materials salvaged from the wrecked *Sea Venture* and named them *Patience* and *Deliverance*. Gates and his castaway men, after spending about eleven months in Bermuda, set sail for Jamestown aboard their newly built ships. Expecting a cheerful welcome upon their long delayed arrival at Jamestown, instead they landed on a 'tumbled-down ghost town'. He was received by the 'skin-and-bones' remnants of the colonists who cried aloud: 'we are starved, we are starved.' A dispirited Gates tried to pick up the pieces of Jamestown, but it was indeed a lost game. Three years after it was settled, Jamestown had failed. About sixty surviving embittered settlers 'made pitch and tar to caulk the *Deliverance, Patience, Discovery* and *Virginia*, and baked bread for the long voyage home...and set sail for England, watching their brief and disastrous American experiment fade from view as they sullenly drifted downstream.'

1610. The home-bound fleet of ships anchored for the night alongside Hog Island, on the right bank of the James. The next morning a boat came upstream bringing the message that English ships with fresh supplies, food and some 300 settlers had arrived at the mouth of the James, under the leadership of the new governor, Thomas West. That was a turning point in American history.

West directed the entire group of deserters to turn back or face prosecution for breaking their settlement contract with the Virginia Company. Twenty-four hours after leaving the 'moribund colony', the embittered survivors were forced to make a new beginning. Governor West had unchallenged authority to expand his domain in the New World 'to include all lands two hundred miles north of Point Comfort, two hundred miles to the south and north-east and from there as far as the Pacific ocean'. That was about 80,000 square miles of eastern North America, or about one-third of the entire continent.

Significantly, among the returnee survivors of the deserted colony, there was a person called John Rolfe, a Bermuda castaway. Arriving back at Jamestown, Rolfe, who had lost his wife and daughter at Bermuda, had no idea how to start his life afresh. While other colonists died dime a dozen around him, or tried their best to find gold to mine or to plant olive, Rolfe tried his hand in growing *apooke*, the wild variety of tobacco smoked by the native Indians. For two years, he experimented with the 'wild weed', to domesticate the unruly *rustica*, but it continued to taste bitter. Meanwhile, Rolfe married the native princess charming, the teenage daughter of Powhatan chief, Pocahontas, who

An 1850s painting of John Rolfe and Pocahontas.

was 'once fascinated by John Smith' and later on 'preferred English ways to the woodland culture'. This first recorded marriage of an Englishman to a native woman raised the hopes on both sides for improved relations and ushering in years of relative peace. Rolfe learned from his Native in-laws some delicate techniques of planting and curing tobacco. The quality of his product improved a lot, but not enough to compare with the mild and superior variety of the Spanish stuff. Rolfe was almost about to give up his experimentation with tobacco when he persuaded a friend, a shipmaster bound for Trinidad, to get hold of some tobacco seeds from there and bring them back for him to Jamestown. This was a bold attempt, since Spain had earlier declared death penalty to anyone selling or providing Spanish tobacco seeds to a non-Spaniard. The year was 1611, Rolfe 'succeeded in creating a unique flavour for Virginian tobacco' combining native skill with Spanish seeds. The trial shipment of his first crop to England in 1613 was instantly singled out for its 'fragrant odour' by the connoisseurs. Encouraged by this response, Rolfe personally took his first commercial shipment of Virginia tobacco to London, accompanied by his native wife, Pocahontas, who had been baptised as Rebecca. Both the native princess and the shipment of Virginia tobacco received a grand public reception at London. Unfortunately, perhaps due to inhospitable English environment for a native Indian, Pocahontas fell ill and died at the tender age of twenty-one. Rolfe returned to Jamestown alone, though with lots of money.

In the wake of Rolfe's success, a boom time of tobacco plantation followed along the Chesapeake Bay settlements. It was being grown in every known spare place. The commercial value of Virginia tobacco was apparent and the patrons at home in England 'needed little persuasion to finance its cultivation'. As the demand for more cultivable land for tobacco grew, the colonists attacked, plundered and pushed back the native tribes from their time-honoured settlements to reclaim their land, to the obvious antagonism of the natives towards the foreign intruders. By 1618, the Jamestown colonists had shipped two thousand pounds of tobacco to their home land that fetched a market price of three shillings a pound 'at a time when that was roughly equal to two days' wages for a common labourer'. In 1622, despite a retaliatory attack by the natives that killed nearly one third of the colonists, sixty thousand pounds of Virginian tobacco were shipped to the home land. By 1627, the shipment totalled 500,000 pounds and it was tripled

An eighteenth century advertisement for Virginia tobacco showing black children working in the fields.

two years later. Finally the colonists were in a position, to compete with the Spanish stuff in the English market.

Tobacco, indeed, saved the Jamestown experiment. But the success story of tobacco was beset with new problems. Shortage of man power. Tobacco planting was extremely labour intensive and despite a continuous inflow of immigrants from the home land, the mortality rate among them was too high. The scarcity of labour became a matter of great concern for the future. The problem was, however, solved by a chance incident. In 1619, a Dutch trading ship dropped anchor in Chesapeake Bay. The ship's cargo, among others, included a batch of 'negars' or African slaves. The colonists bought twenty of them, in 'exchange of tobacco' to work in their fields. Sensing a promising market in slave trade, the Dutch traders returned in subsequent years with more slaves for sale, and slavery quickly became essential to the colony's economy. In a way, tobacco became a major factor for the introduction of slavery to North America. Around the middle of the eighteenth century, about 53,000 slaves were working as tobacco growers in Virginia itself. Out of a total population of about 168,000 in 1753, close to forty per cent were dark-skinned. A few tobacco historians, including Stephen Ambrose surmised: 'If there had been no weed … there would have been no slaves.' The white men were, indeed, getting worried: 'if slaves one day came to outnumber them.' That is another story, of the eventual emergence of civil rights activism for the blacks, or the underprivileged people of the up-and-coming American social superstructure.

With slaves to help and work hard, tobacco, indeed, brought 'gold' and prosperity to the settlers of Jamestown

This 1670 painting shows enslaved Africans working in the tobacco sheds of a colonial tobacco plantation.

and it transformed into a 'stable and civilised' place. The Virginia tobacco, as described by a contemporary poet, 'sweeter than the breathe of fairest maid' became a 'mainstay of tavern and parlour life' in England, propelling enough disposable income for the colonists. In the absence of reliable currency in the colony, the brown leaf 'became a form of money' and some affluent colonists were known to have paid 120 pounds of 'best of leaf tobacco' for eleven 'young maids to make wives'. A hearty meal at a tavern would cost ten pounds of tobacco and eight pounds would fetch a gallon of beer. Virtually anything, including fabrics for clothing, implements for farming, books of verse or on religion, fire arms, even maids for wives, could be obtained for the right amount of Virginia leaf. Clergies, soldiers, and at a given point of time, taxes to local bodies, were paid in terms of tobacco. Besides the crop and currency, tobacco was now 'a way of life in every British colony of the New World'.

*The Lorillard Hogshead in 1789 featuring a
Native American smoking.*

The enterprising citizens of Jamestown went a step further, and unobtrusively indeed, 'introduced the notion of independence' to America by creating a General Assembly, with legislative powers. Its first law was that tobacco should not be sold for less than three shillings per pound. Significantly, the economic boom and stability of Jamestown came at a time when King James had almost lost patience with his New World colony and was about to abandon 'this benighted part of the world'. Had that been so, perhaps, the entire land that would one day become the United States of America, 'might have had French roots or Spanish roots or roots of some other European empire'. It would have been an inconceivably different place altogether. John Rolfe's transformation of tobacco from 'bitter to mild, from burden to boon' lay the cornerstone of the edifice that would one day be known as the mighty United States of America.

1622. By this time, the English had built some fifty farms and dozens of smaller settlements along the banks of the James River, with absolute control over a wide tract of prime land from the Chesapeake Bay to the falls near present-day Richmond. The settlers replaced woods and meadows with tobacco fields, as the natives watched with dismay that 'the territory their distant ancestors had occupied for centuries taken over by the *tassantassas*', the trespassers. The colonists on their part, in order to integrate the natives into the 'English customs and ways' set up a sprawling college in Henricus on a ten thousand-acre land. But contrary to expectations, it further sowed the seeds of suspicion among the natives about the ulterior motives of the unwarranted settlers. The peace process earlier initiated by the Pocahontas—Rolfe marriage was gradually disintegrating with the 'growing marginalisation of the native tribes'. The dormant feeling of distrust and suspicion came out in the open, when in early March 1622, the natives killed an Englishman, owner of a medium-sized tobacco plantation. In retaliation, the colonists killed a popular Native Indian hero, Nemattanow, 'affectionately called Jack of the Feather'. That was, apparently, the last straw of patience and indignation for the natives. On March 22, the Good Friday, they swept down on a plantation near Jamestown, killing about 350 settlers, women and children et al. One of the victims was stated to be John Rolfe. The Virginia governor, Francis Wyatt, by way of reprisal to the native onslaught, initiated an operation for the 'expulsion of the savages', setting 'about a series of missions, razing Indian villages, killing indigenous people, and destroying their crops, deliberately targeting their chief source of food'. By 1640, most of the Virginian natives were wiped out altogether.

1624. Back in London, the happenings in the New World colony sounded the death knell for the Virginia Company. In 1624, King James dissolved the Virginia Company, the commercial operation that had led to the establishment of Jamestown, and assumed royal jurisdiction. King James, though not a lover of tobacco, knew how to profit from it. The King's first decision was to ban growing of tobacco on the soil of his kingdom and ruled out purchasing of the 'weed' from Spain. He further directed that 'from now on all tobacco smoked by Englishmen would be provided by Jamestown', and all Jamestown tobacco had to be shipped to England and to no other markets. Furthermore, it was left to the Crown to set the price of tobacco, and all 'costs related to shipping, freight, insurance, handling, inspection, storage', to be borne by the Jamestown suppliers. The King, indeed, found a way to replenish the Royal Exchequer by gobbling up the New World's new found Brown Gold. Some historians consider this as New World's first tax. There was no compensation guaranteed to Jamestown suppliers, in the event of loss due to shipwreck at sea or if a warehouse was looted or burned. For the King, the New World colony was nothing but a wholly owned subsidiary of the Monarchy, and the colony had no right 'to make its own decisions'.

The Jamestown citizens were stunned by the King's arbitrary decisions. Initially, they wondered whether there had been a mistake, or a miscommunication of some sort. The settlers soon reacted sharply by venting their anger through the monarch's agents. They argued that it was unwarranted to make it mandatory to ship all their exports to England, since from commercial point of view, it was necessary to keep a portion of their product to be reserved for other countries to help advertise the quality of their leaf and to stimulate higher price. They further demanded that the English merchants receiving the tobacco shipment should split the cost evenly with them, maybe even pay more than half the cost, since they were making more than half the profits. And finally, the prices decreed by the King was ludicrously low and unprofitable.

King James would have none of it. The colonists began to rumble. They met in small groups during private hours and talked openly of their discontent with the monarch and his court, something they had never done before. The fallout of the situation perforce resulted in bribery, smuggling and augmentation of profit by adulteration. Customs officials were bribed to allow shipment of tobacco to proceed to places other than England, or some would sail their ships a long way round to avoid official vigil. Reportedly, the Jamestown planters, to augment their profit margin, were adulterating the tobacco meant for English ports with 'salt, straw, dirt, ground glass, paper, garbage and sometimes even the faecal matter of animals'. No one seemed to notice all this, since it was assumed that 'a man who craves for his leaf is not a man to make fine distinctions'.

From Jamestown, soon the rumblings against authoritarian and arbitrary decrees, and undemocratic taxation imposed by the Monarch spread to New World colonies like Maryland, South Carolina, Pennsylvania, Rhode Island and other places. The uncooperative, rather, the rebellious attitude of the colonists incensed the English monarchs from James I to George III, who continued to impose levies and export duties, not only on tobacco, but also on other crops, particularly, on molasses, which raised the price of the colonists' indispensable beverage: rum. On top of it, the Crown also demanded the colonists to provide living quarters, beverages, candles and transportation for the British troops stationed in America. The colonists had obvious grounds to resent such draconian diktats from the Crown.

1773. The resentment and confrontation with the Crown took a dramatic turn at the historic Boston Tea Party, when entire chests of an East India Company shipment of tea were thrown away at sea in the Boston harbour, to protest against the imposition of tea monopoly on the colonists. The rumblings against the autocratic British Crown turned into a revolution, under the aegis of tobacco barons like George Washington, Thomas Jefferson, Patrick Henry and others. Thirteen North American colonies revolted and signed a Declaration of Independence on 4 July 1776, ushering in a free United States of America. On the fractious issue of 'slavery' however, America witnessed a bitter North—South civil war (1861–1865), followed by a great era of reconstruction of the United States of America, and emergence of legendary American civil rights activist, Martin Luther King. The history of those epoch-making happenings in the western hemisphere began in 1611, when the 'gold' sprouting seeds of tobacco were sowed on the soils of Jamestown by an unsung colonist named John Rolfe.

The Globalisation

D R NICOLAS BAUTISTA Monardes (1493–1588), a botanist from Seville and physician to King Philip of Spain, returning from an exploratory expedition to the New World, published a pamphlet, *Historica medicinal de las cosas que se traen de neustras Indias Occidentales* (1565), eulogising the healing properties of the New World's wonder herb: tobacco. Dr Monardes' pamphlet was not only 'an exposition of tobacco's benign effect upon the human brain, which it cleared and invigorated', it also listed an astounding range of maladies that could be cured by the wonder herb. For instance, people with 'short wind', 'griefs of the breast', rottenness at the mouth, bad breath, kidney stones, tape worms, any kind of illness of the intestinal organs, toothache, dandruff, wounds from poison arrows and even tiger bites. He further claimed that the herb could heal 'cattle of new or rotten wounds, maggot infection or any parasite that might trouble the animal'. He refuted the plebeian belief of the 'demonic connection' of tobacco as 'devil's herb' and asserted 'tobacco had the useful satanic qualities of suppressing hunger, curing insomnia and enhancing endurance'.

Dr Monardes' pamphlet provoked a wave of interest across Europe. It was translated into Latin, French, Italian and English. The English version was titled: *Joyful News of Our Newe Founde Worlde*. The French version of the pamphlet was dedicated to the French Queen Catherine de Medici by its translator. The engraving of a tobacco plant, as a frontispiece, was captioned 'Herba Medici', as a sales gimmick, to exploit the goodwill of the Queen's fondness for snuff-tobacco.

In the wake of Dr Monardes' dissertation, followed by the King of Spain's interest in the plant and the French Queen's fascination for the snuff-tobacco, soon the European kings and courtiers were found to be scrambling for the seeds of the 'wonder' plant to be grown in their gardens and backyards as a prized exhibit. It promptly found its way into the elite and royal gardens of Italian and German states, into Switzerland and the Lowlands, and even to the gardens of the Vatican. Initially, it flourished in the European gardens 'in the strength of its appearance alone', and 'was studied and nurtured by court physicians', and was essentially treated as a medicinal plant like other herbs. The French used it to ward off illnesses and preserve beauty. Italians used it in the manner as advised by the priests, and in Switzerland, it was first tested on a dog before being recommended for human use. The Germans, on the other hand, declared it a 'violent herb'. The Englishmen, however, had a different justification for tobacco use: pleasure.

Envisaging the vast potentiality of retail trade in tobacco, the Spanish monarchy founded the *Tabacalera*, in 1636, the world's first tobacco company. State shops were set up to market the company's tobacco products, collecting an additional tax of 3 *reals* per pound. Venice and France had also earlier imposed customs duty on tobacco in 1626 and 1629 respectively. The English King James I had taxed tobacco as early as in 1604. Gradually, most of the European countries introduced some sort of taxation on tobacco products, imports, or consumption. Incidentally, it provided an increasing stream of income to the European governments to finance the devastating internecine conflict between various European nations, 'provoked by religious differences or imperialism', known to the annals of history as the Thirty Years' War (1618–1648), which irrevocably changed the map of Europe. The 'blessed' war not only changed the map of Europe, but it was also instrumental in spreading the tobacco habit to countries as far as Sweden and Russia by the soldiers, merrily flaunting their tobacco gears. The Russians got their first taste of tobacco through the English merchants and mercenary soldiers who carried it in their baggage into that country. The protestant Netherlands, displayed their solidarity with their protestant English ally of the Thirty Years' War, in a rather unique way. As liberalisation flourished in both countries, the 'pleasure of smoking' grew its roots. Tobacco formed a protestant bond for the Dutchmen, who 'favoured the pipe as a tobacco delivery system in imitation of the English' and soon, it became a national brand throughout the Lowlands. A Dutchman without a pipe was almost a national impossibility. It was believed, 'If Dutchman were deprived of his pipe and tobacco, he would not even enter paradise with a glad heart.'

Interestingly, during the outbreak of the great bubonic plague in London in 1665–66, the epidemic, it was claimed, spared the lives of those who were habitual smokers of tobacco. The Prussian King Frederick William I, father of Frederick the Great, was known to be an avid pipe smoker. He was seldom seen without a pipe and his subjects called him the 'smoking King'. His weekly assemblage of advisers, all of them being pipe smokers, was mockingly known as '*tabaks-collegium* or smoking parliament'. The seventeenth century indeed signified a sensational craze for tobacco in the European scene, both as a medicinal herb as well as a 'pleasure' habit.

The myriad avatars of tobacco, originating in the shores of the New World, and after mesmerising the 'civilised' people of Old World European continent, were soon to turn into an international phenomenon. The discovery of the sea-route to India by Vasco de Gama was an open sesame for the venturesome European colonists to spread their wings across Africa, Asia and Far Eastern regions, in their quest for the much sought-after spices and the fabled oriental treasures.

The Portuguese were the earliest among the European nations to set sail on to the exciting waters of the East, setting up trading posts or corporate colonies in Africa, India, and as far as Malacca, the famed Indonesian 'Spice Island'. Spain spread its wings further down to the Malaya archipelago, capturing an island nation comprising 7,017 islands and naming it after their King Philip II as '*Las Islas Filipinas*', what we know today as Philippines. Spain and Portugal were in a way responsible for the introduction of smoking in Africa and Asia as 'a seaman's habit'.

After Vasco de Gama's historic circumnavigation of the globe in 1497–99, the Portuguese took control of the ancient Arab trading stations in Sofala, Mombasa, and Hormuz, and created their own chain of trading posts on Africa's west coast and introduced tobacco to every tribal settlement that they came across. Initially, supplies came from the Portuguese colony in Brazil, but by the end of the sixteenth century tobacco was being cultivated throughout equatorial Africa. The Africans, who were known to be habitual smokers of cannabis, took to tobacco smoking, using their traditional pipe called *dagga*, made of the horn of *ambi* or antelope, and other indigenous smoking gadgets. India, the ancient land of *tamrakuttah or dhumapatrakam or tamakhu*, the Vedic medicinal herb, got the first taste of commercial tobacco via Portuguese settlements in Goa from where it swiftly spread throughout the sub-continent. By the time of Mughal Emperor Jahangir (1569–1627) and later Mughals, the consumption of tobacco had become an acceptable habit among the Indian nobility and the commoners as well. By the middle of the sixteenth century, the Portuguese started cultivation of tobacco in their colony in India, Macao (or Macau), and in their settlements in the East, to meet their ever-growing homeland needs, for barter or for gifts.

The Spanish began cultivation of tobacco in Philippines by about 1575 and from there it spread to Java, China, Japan and Korea. Reportedly, Japan had originally received tobacco courtesy a Spanish shipwreck off its coast in 1542, and the Samurai knights as well as the upper strata of Japanese society took to smoking with an 'unthinking gusto'. They used 'ornate silver tobacco pipes which they strapped to their backs or tucked into their kimonos beside their legendary swords'. A contemporary Nagasaki doctor reported: 'Of late a new thing has come into fashion called "tobacco" which consists of large leaves which were cut up and that one drinks and smokes.' The plant also received Japan's imperial approval and the seeds were sowed and raised in the royal garden in Kyoto. In Korea, interestingly, the plant was called *Nampankoy*, derived from *Nañbañ* or 'Southern Barbarians', a nomenclature perhaps attributed to the 'Portuguese at Macao or the Spaniards in the Philippines', who were presumably responsible for the introduction of tobacco in that country.

From the Portuguese trading post of Macao, tobacco found its way into China. The Chinese initially accepted it as a protection against malaria, a rampant disease in the province of Yunan. Almost the whole population of the area was suffering from malaria, except one battalion that indulged in tobacco smoking. This prompted the people to take to tobacco smoking as an antidote to the deadly disease and thereby everyone, young and old alike, became habitual smokers. The Chinese concept of the medicine *yin* signified 'hot' as a cure for troubles due to cold and moisture, and smoking being a 'hot' pursuit, it promptly motivated the people to take up smoking. Some even preferred smoking against wine and tea as an aid to digestion. In some parts of China, tobacco was known as *Tanbako (tam-ba-ku)*, almost identical to Sanskrit *tamakhu*. It was however not clear how the Chinese adopted the term into their vocabulary.

In due course, China became a conduit for dissemination of tobacco culture to Mongolia, Tibet, Eastern Siberia, Turkestan and South East Asian countries like Vietnam, Burma and Malaya. To the Vietnamese it was promoted as 'health' merchandise. The traders 'dyed it red, the colour of success, before shipping it to Saigon for sale'. In Burma, it was sold as a strength giving 'medicine' and soon became a popular habit among both sexes. The Burmese women 'nourished their children with alternate sucks from the teat and *cheroot* in the belief that a peaceful infancy enabled a child to develop strength'. The Malays believed that tobacco was created in China 'by a fortunate union of dragon and a snake'.

Close on the heels of the Portuguese and Spaniards in the eastern scene, came the Dutch with a vengeance. Comparatively a new vibrant European nation, imbued with 'nationalism and militarism', they quickly took over most of Portugal's trading stations in Africa and Asia, and created new outposts of their own. Roundabout the middle of the seventeenth century, the Dutch were directly dealing with Africans, Arabs, Indians, Ceylonese, Indonesians, and the Chinese, and had established a monopoly on European trade with Japan. The tobacco-savvy Dutch appreciated tobacco's value as an instrument of exchange. A Dutch trade executive observed: 'If we had no tobacco there would hardly be any trade…tobacco could be exchanged for food, ivory, silk, spices and slaves at a very profitable rate.' The Dutch were known to have purchased the entire peninsula of the Cape of Good Hope for a certain quantity of tobacco and wine.

Like the Portuguese and the Spaniards, the Dutch too encouraged tobacco cultivation in the Far East to meet the growing demand for the weed in their home land, as well as for a thriving European market. Tobacco grown in their Jaffna (Ceylon, now Sri Lanka) settlement was a hit, and the Dutch were shipping the Jaffna grown tobacco to Europe as early as in 1625. Ceylon had had its tryst with tobacco even before the arrival of the Dutch and the local Tamil 'enthusiastic smokers' were found to be smoking a 'slender form of cigar' locally called *shuruttu*, meaning 'to roll'. According to some tobacco historians, the rolled-up cigar, called *cheroot*, was presumably derived from the Tamil *shuruttu*.

Batavia in Indonesia became the hub of Dutch trading activities in the South East, and from there tobacco spread to those areas which had not received the weed from Spanish, Portuguese or local trade. The Dutch adopted ingenious techniques in marketing their tobacco products. The betel-

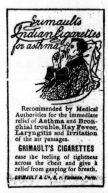

An advertisement for Grimault's Indian Cigarettes, published in the Ceylon Standard, *June 8, 1907.*

nut crazy Balinese were persuaded to chew tobacco on the assurance that the weed would clean their teeth. The Javanese, who were addicted to cloves were provided tobacco mixed with cloves and the locals were made to belief that the 'crackling noise' made while smoking it would ward off evil spirits and bring good fortune to the smoker. With tobacco as a valuable asset, the Dutch soon became masters of the Tropic of Cancer.

In the south-eastern fringe of the globe, there was a landmass vaguely known to the world as the 'Southern Land of Holy Spirits' or the 'Unknown land of the South', inhabited by migrant Asian aboriginals for thousands of years. Until about the beginning of the eighteenth century, the indigenous people of this landmass were peacefully living in harmony amidst wild vegetation and animals, and were known to be chewing cured leaves of a wild weed called *pituri*, to alleviate their hunger as well a cure for several ailments. The wild weed, considered to possess high 'mood-enhancing' properties was an important indigenous trading commodity, and symbolised 'social bonding' as a means of overture for friendship. Then the Macassan fishermen arrived from Indonesia to the shores of this 'unknown' landmass, in search of pearls and *trepan* (a kind of sea cucumber, a Chinese delicacy), a lucrative source of export trade to China. The Macassans acknowledged indigenous ownership of the land and offered pipes and tobacco and other valued goods as tribute to the local population, in return for access to coastal waters and camping places. The locals were enamoured of the 'mood-enhancing' sensation of tobacco and took to smoking as a 'pleasurable' diversion. But the sporadic supply of tobacco via Macassan fishermen was not enough to turn the smoking habit among the locals into an indulgent practice.

In 1770, Great Britain occupied the eastern half of this southern landmass, and on 26 January 1788, the first British fleet arrived on its shores, on a 'penal transportation' mission, with a load of convicts on board. The sight of the cigar or pipe-smoking mariners, highbrow officials as well as convicts, instilled fresh craving for tobacco among the locals. The off-beat settlers were quick to recognise the indigenous desire for tobacco and liberally offered it to them in exchange for labour, goods and services, and hoped that such inducements would motivate the indigenous occupants of the land to forego their traditional lifestyle, becoming 'complement participants' in the settlement's exploitation. It was a sort of 'mutual exploitation'. The indigenous people craved for tobacco and the settlers needed labour, information, and cooperation, to stabilise their newly acquired colony. Some chroniclers even termed the exercise as a 'civilising' or 'taming' drill for the aboriginals. During the early decades of colonisation, the indigenous people of this 'unknown land of the south' were subjected to brutal manual labour, with the lure of tobacco. Even historians, anthropologists and other researchers collected vital data and anecdotes about the primitive lifestyle or customs of the people of the region in return for tobacco. Soon the enticing effect of tobacco took its toll on the indigenous people. The 'pituri clan' lost their way of life and the yesteryear 'wild weed', since identified with the rustica variety of tobacco, gradually faded away, giving way to the 'civilised' tabacum.

This 'unknown' landmass was what we know today as Australia, the nomenclature, derived from Latin *australis* meaning the 'southern'.

Taking a detour to the Middle East, the erstwhile Ottoman Empire that remained a centre of interaction between the East and the West for about six centuries, until about the end of First World War, we found out that tobacco was introduced to this part of the globe between late sixteenth and early seventeenth century. Yemen first encountered tobacco in 1590 through merchants plying the trade routes of the Indian Ocean, followed by Syria and Egypt, in about 1598. About a year later English sailors and traders brought it to Istanbul, and by early seventeenth century, the Egyptian cultivators themselves were known to be growing tobacco.

Interestingly, a chemical analysis of the samples of hair, soft tissues and bone tissues of seven Egyptian mummies dated 1070 BCE and 395 CE, undertaken at the *Institut fur Anthropologie und Humangenetik,* Munich, detected traces of nicotine as that of tobacco, along with other modern day addictive substances like cocaine and hashish. Tobacco must have found its way into ancient Egypt through possible trade relations with the erstwhile 'Turtle Island', the mythical habitat of the weed, much before the Columbus adventure.

After the 'reintroduction' of commercial tobacco, the Ottomans adopted the pipe and the process of smoking at the same time, like their neighbourhood European brethren. However, the Ottomans came to naturalise the pipe by developing their own unique version of a smoking device. Initially, they were using a long-stemmed pipe made of wood connected to the *hajar*, an earthen container, to hold the burning tobacco, attached to the mouthpiece of the pipe. The length of the pipe varied between four to five feet, some were shorter or even longer than the usual length. It was called *chibouk* or Turkish pipe. Soon the *chibouk* was replaced by *narghil*, the Persian version of the Indian water-pipe called *hookah*. Originating in the Malabar Coast in India, it could have been 'dated millennia back', according to some accounts (and might have been originally called something else), but initial traces of *hookah* were found in North Western Provinces of India and in the western areas of Rajasthan and Gujarat around the middle of the sixteenth century during the Mughal period. The water container or the bowl that formed the base of the *hookah* was crafted out of coconut shell, and the Persians while adopting it called

Chaldean man in traditional Turkish costume holding a rifle and a smoking pipe in Istanbul, Turkey, 1869.

narghil, from the Sanskrit *nariyal* or *narikela,* meaning coconut. Incidentally, though *hookah* was of Indian origin, the nomenclature was an adoption of the Arabic *huqqa,* meaning, small box/jar or water urn, a unique instance of an ancient Indo-Arab and Indo-Persian affinity. It turned out to be the most favourite smoking device throughout the Ottoman Empire, particularly in Iran, Turkey and Egypt.

The ingenious Ottoman smokers improvised the *hookah* or the hubble-bubble, into *shisha,* by replacing the coconut-shell bottom with glass bowls. *Shisha* was the Persian term for 'glass', and it promptly came to refer to the glass-bottomed smoking device. A longish, slender, artistically crafted stem, initially made of wood, subsequently upgraded to metals like iron, silver or even gold, connected the glass bottom with a terracotta or metallic conical container at the top for burning tobacco. A gleaming serpentine hose or pipe was attached to the glass bottom for drawing out the smoke that was channelled through an often flavoured water-filled bowl. With surprising rapidity, *shisha* became a hot smoking fashion throughout the Middle East, along with their traditional coffee house culture. Over the years, globally it became an elite smoking device for the up-and-coming generation, and *shisha* or *hookah* bars turned out to be the most sought after joints, visited by the young or old, men or women alike.

By the 1630s, tobacco was being widely cultivated in Western Anatolia and the Fertile Crescent, covering areas around the Mediterranean Sea, particularly in Levant, as Syria or Eastern Mediterranean countries were then historically known. The cultivation of the weed extended

An advertisement for 'Egyptian Deities' cigarettes, 1919.

even up to southern Iraq, Balkans, southern Palestine and as far as the Nile valley. The Ottoman smokers preferred dark strong 'mountain tobacco' grown in Syria, popularly known as '*latakia*', named after the Syrian port town, Latakia, deemed to be an exclusive home-grown product of the Levant, oblivious to the exotic origin of the leaf. Turkey and Egypt produced a mild variety of tobacco which 'was smooth on intake' and found a ready market in Europe. After the American Revolution, in particular, whenVirginia tobacco became a scarcity in the European market, the continental connoisseurs of smoking turned to the Turkish and Egyptian blends for their daily dosage of 'pleasure'.

In roughly the early part of the nineteenth century, the globalisation of tobacco, or Brown Gold, was complete.

The Fad

CHARLES DICKENS, THE eminent Victorian era English novelist, author of classics like *Oliver Twist*, *A Tale of Two Cities*, *Great Expectations*, and many more, was a great admirer of the American liberation movement. Dickens was anxious to visit the brave new world on the other side of the Atlantic. He was already the most famous living author in the English-speaking world and had many admirers in America because of his meticulous exposure of the prevalent social injustices and 'sarcasm towards Britain's upper classes'. In January 1842, when *Britannia*, with the author on board, anchored in Boston harbour, Dickens was accorded an unprecedented welcome and was virtually mobbed by the newspaper editors to interview the international celebrity and a champion for the cause of the downtrodden. The overwhelmed author of *Great Expectations* was elated with the prospect of great expectations in the land he held in high esteem to 'find a freedom from the corruptions of… social injustice and discredited snobbery that characterised English society.' But, Dickens was in for a shock, soon enough.

One day in New York, Dickens was riding with some friends in a wagon, conversing lightly and enjoying the sights and the bustle of the city. As the vehicle crossed the Broadway, the author looked outside and was startled by the sight of 'a select party of half a dozen gentlemen hogs have just now turned the corner'. The conversation stopped and everyone in the wagon looked out in anguish. A few days later, when the author was travelling in a canal boat through the western states, he encountered even 'more dumbfounding sights', fellow passengers with 'yellow streams from half-chewed tobacco trickling down their chins' and boisterous 'hawking and spitting the whole night through', making it impossible for him to get a wink of sleep. Everywhere he went he saw 'chewing and spitting…indoors and out, at work and at play, among men and women and children…. He saw more spittoons than any other piece of furniture.' But the most depressing sight he encountered was in Washington DC, the seat of the government of the new nation, and wrote back home for his readers:

> 'Washington may be called the headquarters of tobacco-tinctured saliva…. In all the public places of America, this filthy custom is recognised. In the courts of law, the judges had his spittoons, the crier his, the witness his, and the prisoner his; while the jurymen and spectators are provided for…. In the hospitals, the students of medicine are requested by notices upon the wall, to eject their tobacco juice into the boxes provided for that purpose…. In public buildings, visitors are implored, through the same agency, to squirt the essence of their quid or "plug", as I have heard them called by gentlemen

learned in this kind of sweetmeat, into the national spittoons, and not about the bases of the marble columns.... The stranger will find (the custom) in its full bloom of glory, luxuriant in all its alarming recklessness, at Washington.'

Dickens, himself a tabagophile, 'a cigar after dinner when I am alone', being his favourite smoking habit, summarised his impressions about chewing and spitting habits of the Americans of that time as 'the most sickening, beastly and abominable custom that ever civilisation saw'.

It was a subject of historical debate why a nascent nation took to chewing tobacco, while the rest of the world, particularly Old World Europe adopted smoking as a favourite pastime. Eric Burns, a tobacco historian observed, '... Americans needed unoccupied hands. They had the machines of the Industrial Revolution to operate, as well as plows to steer, trees to clear, homes to build, oars to stroke, livestock to feed, reins to pull, games to shot, corps to raise, livestock to feed, tools to sharpen, and a host of other activities of one sort of another to pursue.... The plug was, in short, the perfect tobacco for the people who were constructing a nation form the scratch.' Around the time of the Civil War, Americans 'chewed far more than they lit'. Out of about 350 tobacco factories listed in Virginia and North Carolina in 1860, only seven were known to be producing tobacco for pipe blends. The chewing tobacco was generally flavoured with rum, nutmeg, tonka beans, sugar, cinnamon, liquorice and honey, and was marketed under brand names like, *Live and Let Live, Buzz Saw, Barbed Wire,*

Bull of the Woods and lastly, *Beat the Dickens*, apparently to counter the English author's calamitous comments on the contemporaneous American habit of chewing tobacco.

During the presidency of Andrew Jackson (1829–1837) 'chewing tobacco became a national pastime, the man and the era collaborating perfectly ... to further the cause of hard-pumping jaws and dark brown spittle.' Spittoons were seen everywhere; on public buildings, streets, bars and restaurants, and in almost every corner of the country, as if it was akin to being the national emblem. '*Chaw*', the popular American term for chewing tobacco, found a rapturous reference in the famed American author, Samuel Clemens aka Mark Twin's famous work, *Adventures of Huckleberry Finn*:

> '... there was as many as one loafer leaning up against every awning post, and he always had his hands in his britches pockets, except when he fetched out to "lend a chaw of tobacco or to scratch. What a body was hearing amongst them, at all the time was—
>
> "Gimme a chaw 'v tobacker,- Hnak."
>
> "Cain't – I hain't got but one chaw left. Ask Bill."
>
> May be Bill gives him a chaw; maybe be lies and says he ain't got none. Some of them kinds of loafers never has a cent in the world, nor a chaw of tobacco of their own. They get all their chawing by borrowing....'

Chewing tobacco and spitting was such an obsession with the Americans that they would vie for the honour of spitting the longest distance. Even as late as in the mid-forties of the twentieth century, 'tobacco squirting' contests were held in North Carolina. Reportedly, a most energetic 'juice flinger', in a 1946 tournament, failed to match the record of a 'long-distance squirt of twenty-one feet two inches achieved by the 1945 champion'.

By the end of the nineteenth century, the American fad of chewing tobacco had gradually faded away, Finally, in 1945, the US District Court at Washington ordered the removal of 'cuspidors' from all federal buildings, and the New York City Board of Health notified that it was no longer mandatory for bars and other public places to maintain 'the homely spittoons' for public use. However, Iain Gately surmises that 'the once national American habit of chewing tobacco still survives in the mass mastication of gum, whose purpose, interestingly, is perceived of as being to extract toxins and purify the chewer, just as tobacco had promoted the lung-cleansing habit of spitting.'

Chewing was the oldest form of tobacco use, dating from the primordial days of our nomadic ancestors' 'eat and find out' explorations in search of edible vegetation. Even Mayans were known to have been chewing tobacco mixed with lime. Some South American natives were known to be using tobacco juice as a weapon to 'blind an enemy' by furiously spurting the juice towards them. The tactic, indeed, demanded furious mastication of tobacco inside one's mouth to generate 'the explosive force of a guided missile and superb marksmanship'. The Spaniard invaders, when they landed in Paraguay in 1503, were known to have encountered similar attacks from the natives, splattering 'their faces and stinging their eyes and fouling their clothes'. The invaders perforce had to withdraw in confusion and disgust.

During the early period of colonisation, the transatlantic European sailors, even though they preferred smoking, took to chewing tobacco 'to eliminate the risk of fire on a wooden ship', as well as to keep 'their hands free so that they could enjoy their weed at the same time that they did the ship's work'. The transatlantic sailors chewed tobacco at every port, spreading the habit wherever they went.

Initially, tobacco mastication was introduced in Europe as a dentifrice and for other therapeutic values. In England, the soldiers were initiated into the chewing habit courtesy the famed Stuart General, George Monck, a 'plug' addict. The habit slowly trickled down to the common man, as well among English literary circle. Eulogistic verses on the quid, *An Old Maid That Chewed Tobacco* by Francis Hoyland, and *Elegy on a quid of Tobacco* by Robert Southey, and many more, were indicative enough of the chewers' popularity in eighteenth century England.

Europeans had given up the habit of tobacco chewing by the end of the eighteenth century, and 'spittoons, or spits, were seldom seen in the Old World except at the bedside of invalids'. However, nineteenth century Europe witnessed the spread of a different kind of tobacco product for oral consumption: *snus* (not to be confused with snuff). Developed in Sweden in the early eighteenth century, snus was a kind of moist tobacco powder for placing under the upper lip for a prolonged period of time and did not require spitting. The Swedes preferred *snus* over smoking. The habit was quickly adopted by the neighbouring countries: Norway, Finland and Denmark, and by the end of the nineteenth century, it became a widespread habit throughout Europe. *Ettan*, meaning 'number one', the branded Swedish *snus*, packaged in attractive containers, found a ready market not only in Europe, but also was exported to USA and Canada.

Coincidentally, in many ways, Swedish *snus* and its consumption pattern resembled the Indian variant, *khaini* and *gutka*. *Khaini* was dry powdered tobacco mixed with lime, and *gutka* was a preparation of crushed areca nut (betel nut), tobacco, catechu, paraffin, slacked lime and sweet or savoury flavourings. Both these Indian tobacco products were meant for oral consumption by putting a pinch of the substance between the gum and cheek. The quid dissolved inside the mouth with the outflow of saliva, turning it deep red in colour. It supposedly created a 'mood enhancing' sensation, subdued the feeling of hunger, sharpened the level of mental alertness, and generated a sustainable energy.

Unlike Swedish *snus*, both the *khaini* and *gutka* consumers are required to expel the excess saliva generated inside the mouth. Thus, spitting at regular intervals became an inevitable habit for the addicts of these indigenous tobacco products, and they did so at will anywhere and everywhere, spattering the dark red toxic spittle on the base of public buildings, monuments, staircases of buildings, or on any conceivable or unconceivable objects, defacing them unashamedly. The compulsive spitters did not even spare the historic and fashionable Connaught Place shopping arcade in New Delhi, and according to a survey report, jeopardised the massive steel foundation of Calcutta's iconic Howrah Bridge across the river Hooghly. If 'spittoons' were like the 'national emblem' for nineteenth century America, 'spitting' continues to be an Indian 'national character' even in the twenty-first century.

It was not precisely known how or when *khaini* and *gutka* originated, though it has been known to be a prevailing habit in India since long. The origin of *gutka* could perhaps be traced to a traditional Indian custom of chewing *paan* (betel leaf) rolled with aromatic herbs and granulated areca nuts as mouth freshener after every meal. During the Mughal period, the pleasure-seeking Muslim aristocracy improvised the *paan* roll by adding flavoured tobacco granules to create an aura of sensuality and satiety. From the mansions of Muslim noblemen, the custom spread to the common man, becoming a mass habit eventually that is prevalent even today. As of today, with mechanised mass production, easy availability at a low price, supported by 'push' marketing, and available in attractively designed pouches (costing .50 paise to Re 1.00 or 2.00 per pouch), *gutka* has turned out to be a favourite pastime for a wide spectrum of people, high or low class, young or old, or men or women, for the quick 'high' it generates at a minimal cost.[1] The antecedents

---

[1] On the basis of medically proven evidence about the existence of oral cancer causing chemicals in the smokeless tobacco products like *gutka*, *khaini*, etc., the Government of India banned the sale of all chewing tobacco products throughout the country. So far twenty-six Indian states and union territories have implemented the ban, though clandestine sale and consumption of the products go on unabated.

of *khaini* could not be traced out, though it was an equally rampant habit among Indians. The etymologically-inclined readers might be interested to know that the term *khaini* is a Hindi word, meaning quid of tobacco. *Gutka* was seemingly derived from Sanskrit *gutika,* meaning granules.

By the eighteenth and early nineteenth centuries, while the practice of smoking was circumnavigating the globe, America was chewing tobacco and spitting at will, whereas France was snuffing and sneezing with gusto as a national habit. Ever since French Queen Catherin de Medici took to snuff to sneeze out her nagging migraine, snuff had not only become a hot favourite with the French noblemen, the Frenchmen picked up the habit with an uncanny exuberance, and soon the whole of Europe was also sneezing. In the mid-eighteenth century, 'the French were considered to be the most witty and stylish race in Europe. Their philosophy, literature and manners were widely imitated.' Imitating the French, the eighteenth century Europeans, particularly the Englishmen, switched to snuffing, despite the on-going predominance of smoking, as an alternative mode of a 'pleasure' ritual.

'Snuffing, like enlightenment, was a French invention… while snuffing was practiced from Andes to the Scottish glens, it took the French to make a fashion out of it…it had been a (French) court habit since the days of Jean Nicot.' Though the French were credited with the introduction of snuff as a fashion in Europe, it was the Spanish and Portuguese settlers in the New World, particularly in South America, who first came across the indigenous ritual of sniffing powdered tobacco. Spanish Monk Ramon Pane, a shipmate of Columbus on his second voyage to the New World, recoded that the Natives were 'snuffing through a tube, one end placed over the powdered leaf and the other through in the nose, and so drawn up, which purges them very much.' Europeans in the Spanish and Portuguese colonies adopted tobacco snuffing, sans tube, as another New World 'curiosity' like that of smoking or chewing

Around the early sixteenth century, limited medicinal use of snuff was observed in Lisbon and in some other parts of Spain. Spanish and Portuguese clergy were known to be 'taking tobacco only in snuff', closely followed by the Italian priests, as a 'less conspicuous' and less hazardous alternative. Father Joseph Desa of Cupertino, a mystic monk of the Order of St Francis, and an avid snuffer, affirmed, 'snuff served to keep him alert for prayers and other holy duties and it restrained carnal desires.'

The process of snuffing was less complex and its effect was almost instantaneous. 'The physiological result of taking a pinch of snuff was a sneeze or a succession of sneezes. The detonation resulting from a charge of tobacco powder to the nose was assumed by enthusiastic snuffers to have salutary value'. It cleared the 'head of superfluous humors invigorated the brain and brightened the eyes'. The evident enjoyment was 'psychosomatic'.

Climbing down the holy altars of the clergymen and out of the confines of the French Court, this exotic habit began to filter through to the masses of people in Portugal, Spain, Italy and France. The scenario was aptly reflected in the contemporary French playwright Moliere's famous play: *Dom Juan ou Le Festin de pierre,* based on the legendary figure of *Don Juan*. The opening scene of the play showed a character, snuff box in hand, singing in praise of tobacco: 'Whatever Aristotle and all of philosophy might say, there is nothing equal to tobacco: it is the passion of the honest people, and he who lives without tobacco is not worthy of living. Not only does it rejuvenate and purge the human brain, it also instructs the soul on virtue and teaches one to become an honest man....'

In Ireland, the snuff was locally called 'smutchin' and became a widely popular fashion by the middle of the seventeenth century. The Scottish Highlanders were known to be a nation of enthusiastic snuffers and they were pounding tobacco into snuff in their personal mills. '...a figure of a Highlander taking a pinch or holding a snuff mull (a snuffbox of horn)' was considered to be emblematic of Scottish nationalism. In Prussia, Friedrich the Great's edicts against 'careless smoking' compelled the Prussians 'who wished to have a public life and a tobacco habit' to switch over to snuff.

During the early years of the seventeenth century, the Englishmen, particularly in cosmopolitan London, considered snuffing 'to be exclusive to the dandies of France'. Snuffer court favourites of King Charles II were frowned upon by all good Englishmen as a habit 'not worthy of imitation'. However, the English commoners were found to be sneezing with relish as they snuffed 'ground tobacco stalks or worthless leaves'. The English 'poor' men's snuff habit received a boost when the English fleet, after a raid of Cadiz and Vigo in 1702, returned 'with an enormous quantity of superior Havana and Spanish snuffs as part of the prizes of war'. The booty was promptly purchased by the seaport merchants, and disposed of at a low price to the 'land-sharks', who in their turn found a ready market among the 'poor' snuff addicts. The Englishmen were, thereby, 'unexpectedly introduced to exquisitely flavoured "Seville" snuff and the variety known for its scent as musty. As the demand for this exotic variety increased, spurious and less palatable snuff flooded the English market. But, for the *habitué*,' it was the sneeze that mattered and soon sneezing became endemic in the metropolitan towns of England. With the patronage of Queen Anne 'the accepted fashions of the French aristocracy soon became a polite routine at British court.' All the people who mattered, including the English aristocracy, became confirmed snuffers.

Following the French arbiters of fashion, by the middle of the eighteenth century, the English 'polite society' had developed their own unique snuff cult. 'The courtly dandy would offer his box in a gesture which served to display his rings, his lace cuff and his embroidered handkerchief to the best advantage. The box, having being correctly held, the lady or gentleman to whom it was offered would deign to take a pinch. The taker, if a lady, had then an opportunity to exhibit (by studied indirection) her rings, her bracelets, her smooth arm and delicate wrist. The pinch was something to linger over, for a moment. The recommended conversation at this juncture dealt with the virtues of the proffered snuff and an appropriate comment on the container. After the owner of the box had joined in a sniff, the cover was snapped close with military precision. The conversation, punctuated with delicate or hearty sneezes, could then proceed into normal channels of intrigue, the weather or such matters which placed no strain upon the intellect... The mentors of etiquette thus sought to make snuff taking an exclusive attribute of the well-bred.'

The contemporary 'well-bred' English snuffers included personalities like Edward Gibbon, the greatest English historian, who was 'reliant on tobacco for inspiration, consulting his muse via his nose'. As well as Dr Samuel Johnson, the celebrated British lexicographer, who 'took snuff by the fistful and filled the pockets of his coat with the magic tobacco dust'. The 'well-bred' snuffers of the era included Pope Benedict XIII, Frederick the Great, Swedenborg, Robert Burns, Addison, Swift and Napoleon, to name only a few. About Napoleon, it was said: 'he took a kilo of snuff each week, the equivalent to a hundred-a-day cigarette habit.' Talleyrand, a French bishop, politician, diplomat and Napoleon's chief diplomatic aide, declared: 'snuffing was an essential of diplomacy'.

The 'well-bred' and 'polite society' snuff snobbery had another side to the story: craze for snuff boxes, according to the social status of the snuffer. This resulted in the emergence of enterprising entrepreneurs producing fashionable snuff boxes made of platinum, gold, crystal, lead, iron, oyster shells, bones, horns, tusks, ivory, bamboo, gourd, amber and other miscellaneous materials. Seasoned artists and skilled craftsmen were deployed to artistically design, paint and engrave the boxes with scenes of woodlands, seascapes, palatial buildings and even erotic figures. There were snuff boxes for each part of the day and for each season: heavier boxes for winter and lighter for summer. Gifting of snuff boxes became a social grace for the eighteenth century *beau monde*, who took pride in his myriad collection of snuff boxes, rather than 'having a library or a cabinet of natural history'. Napoleon was also known to be a great collector of expensive snuff boxes made of precious metals or ivory. One of his favourite and lucky snuff boxes was engraved with a portrait of his first wife, Josephine, on the lid.

Initially, snuff production was a limited enterprise in Spain and Portugal. Towards the beginning of the eighteenth century, 'production of tobacco powder in many varieties became extensive in these two countries and was an important article of export'. Seville snuff, in particular, became Europe's most sought after product for its aromatic flavours. With growing domestic demands, large scale snuff factories were established in France, western Germany, the Netherlands, Scotland and England. Glasgow exported snuff to the North American British colonies, even though Virginia, New England and New York had already started their own snuff factories around the same time.

In the Middle East, the *ulema* (Muslim religious scholars) were conspicuous snuff takers. They preferred this habit against the fire hazard of smoking or the vexatious exercise of spitting involved in the act of chewing tobacco. Ottoman nomads were also known to be habitual snuff takers and though the habit was not particularly prevalent among the general populace, snuff merchants were known to be operating in Cairo and Giza in the early nineteenth century. In Asia, it was the Jesuit missionaries and Portuguese traders who introduced the snuff habit into China and

Japan and the Portuguese posts in India, though snuff was not altogether unknown in these areas.

China particularly accepted it for its therapeutic value: 'treating cold or inducing sweat'. It, however, soon became a recreational habit in China. The Chinese who had converted to Christianity were labelled 'snuff-takers' because of the practice's Jesuit connection. As the demand grew, China opened their own snuff factories in Canton and Peking, claiming to produce superior quality snuff compared to the imported varieties from Europe. With the gradual infiltration of the custom among the Chinese aristocratic and official level, and a growing snuff cult, Chinese entrepreneurs developed unique containers: snuff bottles, instead of boxes. Eighteenth-century China witnessed a large-scale production of exquisitely designed small snuff bottles made of glass, porcelain, ivory, and jade that were a collector's pride. The stoppers of the bottles usually came attached with tiny ivory spoons.

The French Revolution marked the end of the snuff era in France and Europe, as well as elsewhere. The general public progressively discarded the habit as the custom of anti-people *ancien regime*. The habit lingered on, though with subdued intensity, among the Irish and Scottish public, as well as among some 'stubborn English aristocracy'.

Tobacco historians considered 'it was the English who first made the habit of smoking a national recreation,' and 'discovered pipe smoking and had introduced it to an eagerly receptive world'. Ever since Sir Walter Raleigh dramatically turned 'smoke into gold', lit a pipe for his darling Queen and boasted about the introduction of tobacco to the 'civilised' world, the English adopted smoking with an indomitable zest.

The Elizabethan literati and intelligentsia were enthusiastic in expounding upon the cause of tobacco and smoking in many ways. Christopher Marlow, the playwright and a 'sexual adventurer', author of *Dr Faustus* declared, 'All they that love not boys and tobacco are fools.' Ben Jonson's most successful satirical play, *Every Man in his Humour* had a character, Captain Bobdill, eulogising the value of tobacco: 'I have been in the Indies, where this herb grows, where neither myself, nor a dozen gentlemen more, of my knowledge, have received a taste of any other nutriment in the world, for a space of one and twenty weeks, but the fume of this simple only: therefore, it cannot be, but "its most divine!"…the most sovereign and precious weed, that ever the Earth tendered to the use of man.' Playwright Edmund Spenser hailed 'divine tobacco' in his allegorical poem *Faerie Queene,* dedicated to Queen Elizabeth, while poet Samuel Rowlands, in his poem *Knave of Clubs*, complemented nourishing qualities of the weed. The celebrated Elizabethan era philosopher and scientist Francis Bacon said: 'In our times the use of tobacco is growing greatly and conquers men with a certain secret pleasure, so that those who have once become accustomed thereto can later hardly be restrained therefrom.' Isaac Newton, the great English scientist 'smoked incessantly…from his infancy until his death bed'.

As smoking became *de rigueur* among English socialites, there emerged a new class of people, nicknamed 'reeking gallants'. These people would visit a theatre or a social

gathering with their paraphernalia of pleasure – expensive
tobacco boxes, knives, tong, pipes, and so on, carried
by dedicated servants. The flamboyant 'gallants' were
'expected to possess a lengthy repertoire of tricks involving
a combination of facial contortions and expulsion of
carefully shaped tobacco clouds…the perfect smoke rings'.
The correct use of the pipe for full enjoyment of tobacco
was considered a 'highly exclusive art'. Private clubs and
homes sprang up in London to train people in the art of
'nicotine mannerism' under qualified 'professors of the art
of whiffing', to explain the procedures 'which converted
the simple act of pipe smoking into a bizarre art'. Affluent
Londoners and 'popinjays' vising the city, were regulars to
these 'schools' of 'nicotine mannerism'.

From the beginning, English commoners or 'poor'
people picked up the smoking habit for the medicinal
value of tobacco, particularly as an efficacious cure for
bubonic plague. A European visitor to England observed:
'In England, when children went to school, they carried in
their satchels, with their books, a pipe of tobacco, which
their mother took care to fill early in the morning, it serving
them instead of a breakfast; and at the accustomed hour
everyone laid aside his book to light his pipe, the master
smoking with them, and teaching them how to hold their
pipes and draw in; thus accustoming them to it from their
youth, believing it absolutely necessary for a man's health.'

The protestant Dutch, who took to pipe smoking
with unfailing zeal in imitation of their protestant English
ally, gave vent to their craze for the pipe in a different way.
The seventeenth century Dutch artists 'drew inspiration

from representing the common man indulging in his favourite pastime, i.e. drinking and smoking', and insisted 'in placing pipes in the mouth of most of their subjects… to perpetuate the reputation of the Dutch as smokers *par excellence.*'

While chewing tobacco, taking snuff, smoking the pipe and other smoking devices were predominant in the European world and elsewhere, the tobacco scenario witnessed the emergence of a new fad: cigar.

English traveller John Cockburn, while on his way to Costa Rica, was presented with a *ceegar* (cigar) by a group of Franciscan monks about which he published an account in 1735: 'These gentlemen gave us some *ceegars* to smoke, which they supposed would be very acceptable. These are the leaves of tobacco rolled up in such a manner that they serve both for a pipe and tobacco itself. These, the ladies, as well as gentlemen, are very fond of smoking; but indeed, they know no other way here, for there is no such thing as a tobacco pipe throughout New Spain…' Presumably, Englishmen were not aware of the cigar until about this time.

The Spanish New World colonisers were the first to come across cigar, via the Mayan and Aztec rituals. In their home land, the Spaniards were smoking cigars since the day when Rodrigo de Xerez smoked openly in the streets of his home town Ayamonte, but the fad did had not caught up sufficiently enough. Spanish America's tobacco products, which were specifically shipped to Cadiz and Seville, were mostly grounded into snuff to meet the growing European demand, while a limited quantity was rolled into cigars for domestic consumption.

Once considered to be a crude primitive ritual, the cigar drew the attention of the 'civilised' world via Seven Years' War (1756-1763), the first known global warfare, involving many nations across three continents. Curiously enough, a Massachusetts born farmer, Israel Putnam, or Old Put, as his friends called him, played an interestingly important role to familiarise the cigar to the 'civilised' world. Putnam joined the British army, then fighting against the Spanish-French caucus. In 1762, the British launched a massive onslaught on Cuba. Along with the British forces, Putnam was also shipped off to Cuba, landing in *Vuelta Abajo*, a rich tobacco growing land, to the extreme west of the island. Putnam was, however, very unhappy. Fatigued by the heat of the area, he felt miserable due to the unavailability of his favourite pipe blend. He was dejected and cranky and longed for his peaceful 'Connecticut farm and the kind of weed he savoured'. One of his fellow men suggested that he try the native smoke, a cigar. Putnam refused to trust something which was 'radically different'. There upon another companion said: '... it was either cigar or abstinence for the duration of the war—and who knew how long that would be?' Old Put changed his mind and reluctantly tried one. As he 'drew the smoke into his mouth, felt it infuse him, felt himself warm.' He became an instant convert. He also realised that pipe 'was inappropriate in battle, when man needed to get his smoke going quickly and keep it going, often on the move.'

At the end of the Seven Years' War, Old Put loaded three donkeys with all the Cuban cigars they could carry, along with some tobacco seeds, personally off-loaded them onto his ship, kept a strict vigil on his precious cargo all through the journey back home, to his favourite Connecticut farm. There, 'he introduced his friends to cigar, his friends introduced them to their own friends, and Israel Putnam encouraged them all. He was the first American importer of fine Havana cigars and did for that smoke in his country, although in a smaller scale, what Sir Walter Raleigh had done for the pipe in England many years before.'

After the American Revolution, by 1801, Americans had begun their own commercial production of cigars in South Windsor, Connecticut. Soon thereafter a company in eastern Pennsylvania was producing a product called '*stogie*' – 'a black, twisty, cheap and strong' cigar. Around 1810 twenty-nine million cigars were manufactured in the United States out of which twenty-seven million were produced in Pennsylvania, main centres of production being Philadelphia city and county, essentially to cater to the domestic demands. The new found fad also found its way into contemporary American literature, though in a limited way, compared to the paeans written in Elizabethan England. Emotional references about cigar figured in Stephen Crane's classic civil war novel, *The Red Badge of Courage*, in Willa Cather's *A Lost Lady*, and in the works of novelist Nathaniel Hawthorne.

It was again a war, the Peninsular War (1807–1814), when Spain, Britain and Portugal jointly fought against the First French Empire for the control of the Iberian Peninsula, which was instrumental in spreading the cigar fad in Europe. The 'forced mingling' of soldiers of diverse regions attributed to the spread of the hitherto lesser known smoke dispensing device into European soil. Interestingly, the British 'had concurred the French on Spanish soil', but 'the cigar had conquered them both'. Enamoured Englishmen longed for cigars, but no cigars were then domestically manufactured. Limited domestic production of cigar began in England by the 1820s. As per official records, about 250,000 pounds were being produced by 1830s, though, reportedly, a much larger quantity were being smuggled into England from Spain and Portugal. This was, indeed, a sign of 'swift development of the habit of cigar smoking in England' and a new generation of 'powerful puffers' emerged in England

Cigar smoking became a popular leisure activity of the upper classes in nineteenth century England. Hotels and clubs were building special rooms for smoking, in addition, there were smoking railroad cars. The after-dinner stogie, accompanied by glasses of port or brandy, became a tradition.

'who seemed to feel that pipe tobacco and snuff merely served as an introduction to the greater joy of the unalloyed smoke of cigar'. It was a 'blustering renaissance' in the world of smoke. Cuba producing the hot favourite Havana cigars, while other factories in the West Indies were the largest beneficiaries of the 'renaissance', who were 'shipping considerable quantities of cigars in a variety of shapes and brands to eager European markets', Englishmen, the Dutch and the Germans being the larger consumers.

Besides cigar, the nineteenth century smoking 'renaissance' in Europe witnessed the advent of an oriental delight, the *hookah* from India and the *narghile* of Persia, a unique water-bowl or water-pipe smoking device, generally known as hubble-bubble to the western world. Throughout the Mohammedan world, particularly in Persia, India and the East Indies, it was quite a popular smoking instrument, the upper-crust, in particular, transforming it into an

An illustration from an article on 'The History and Mystery of Tobacco' in Harper's New Monthly Magazine, *1855.*

elaborate 'pleasure' habit. In India '…hookah was firmly established in the Moghul states' and British soldiers and the men at the helm of the newly established empire in the sub-continent adopted the *hookah* cult in a manner reminiscent of the Elizabethan 'reeking gallants'. These pleasure-seeking Englishmen, in imitation of the sensuous local nobles, kept concubines, smoked *hookah* through serpentine *hookah* pipes, ensconcing themselves on comfortable couches, often surrounded by sycophants and employed 'special servants, termed *hookah-burdars* to carry and tend the instrument of their pleasure.' When these gentlemen returned home to England, they carried back with them the legacy of this oriental 'curiosity' that soon attracted the attention of the smokers' coterie not only in England, but also in various parts of Europe.

Consumption of tobacco by way of smoking pipe, cigar or hubble-bubble, or chewing and snuffing, reached the pinnacle of glory by the end of the nineteenth century, particularly becoming an obsession even with the high and mighty politicians and diplomats. In 1871, the great Prussian statesman Bismarck observed: 'a cigar held in hand and nursed with care serves, in a measure, to keep our gestures under control. Besides, it acts as a mild sedative without in any way impairing our mental faculties. A cigar is a sort of diversion: as the blue smoke curl upwards the eye involuntarily follows it; the effect is soothing, one feels better tempered, and more inclined to make concessions – and to be continually making mutual concessions is what we diplomats live on.' The dogged portrait of Winston Churchill with a cigar in his mouth (knowledgeably, he was never seen in public without a cigar in his mouth), which was indeed symbolic of the politian's fascination for cigar, or tobacco consumption in any manner, through to the twentieth century.

Cigar found fervent references in Russian author Turgenev's *A Fire at Sea*, French author Gustave Flaubert's *Madam Bovary,* and English novelist Thackeray's *Vanity Fair*. French writer Stendhal wrote: 'On a cold morning in winter, a Toscan cigar fortifies the soul', while American novelist Nathaniel Hawthorne 'resented regulations stipulating how far one could walk on the Sabbath and that forbade smoking a "seegar" on the street or consuming alcohol.' But, Lord Byron, the great English Romantic Era poet excelled over all of them when he exclaimed:

> Sublime tobacco! Which from east to west
> Cheers the Tar's labour or Sultan's rest,
> Which on Moslem's ottoman divides
> His hours and rivals opium and his brides;
> Magnificent in 'Stamboul, but less grand,
> Though not less loved, in Wapping or the Strand,
> Divine in Hookahs, glorious in a pipe,
> When tipped with amber, mellow, rich and ripe;
> Like other charmers, wooing the caress,
> More dazzling when daring in full dress;
> Yet thy true lovers more admire by far
> Thy naked beauties – give me a cigar!

Meanwhile, quietly a revolution, in the 'world of smoke' was brewing to explode with a bang.

The seed of this revolution can be traced back to the

primordial times. The American Native tribes, while rolling the tobacco leaves into 'muskets', did not use the entire plant. The stems were cut off and the damaged leaves were left out to be eaten by animals or to rot. But soon they began to mend their ways, realising perhaps that it was rather sinful to waste even a small fraction of the 'gift of gods'. They started collecting every small bit of the plant, dried and powdered them to make them into smaller muskets, 'in a piece of reed or bark or straw or sometimes a leaf of maize or a leaf of banana skin packing the tobacco tightly and smoothing off the ends.' The smaller 'muskets' were given for smoking to the people belonging to the lower strata of their social order, the 'very young, the very old, the poor members of the tribe and to women'.

The little muskets were reinvented in Europe, around the beginning of the seventeenth century, and like the primordial tribal practice, as the 'smoke of the outcasts'. The cigar butts, snuff remnants and crusts of tobacco that the 'well-bred' had scraped out of their pipes and thrown away, were collected by the 'poor' or the homeless people who would roll them up into a piece of paper, that too often picked up from the garbage, and smoked them generally at night in their dingy homes, or in some shadowy places. These 'poor' or homeless people never realised that 'the smoke they released on earth would one day take the world by storm'. The Spanish New World explorers were the first to come across this prototype in Mexico and carried the concept back to their country to be revived by its 'poor' and rural population as their smoking habit. Towards the end of the seventeenth century, 'tobacco use had become endemic in Spain', and a large segment of its people in the countryside, following the Aztec notion, consumed their tobacco wrapped in a twist of maize husk. The city dwellers substituted paper for leaves. In Spanish, this unique smoking device was called *papalote* or *cigarillo*, or the little 'paper cigar'.

The tobacco factories in Seville were the first to manufacture the little paper cigars as 'a poor man's by-product of the lordly cigar – scraps of discarded cigar butt wrapped in a scrap of paper', essentially to cut down the cost of producing cigar, snuff or pipe blends. Women workers were employed by these factories, as their nimble fingers were considered aptly suitable to hand-roll the delicate little paper cigars. That was the beginning. Soon the Spanish *papalote* or *cigarillo* made its way to Portugal, Italy, the Levant, South Russia and to the Orient, even as far as in Japan.

During the Napoleonic wars against Spain, while the French soldiers invaded that country, they in their turn were enticed by the slim little Spanish tobacco cylinders. These soldiers, and subsequently the French writers visiting the French occupied Spain, were enamoured of the sight of pretty Spanish girls, working in Spanish tobacco factories, under extremely humid conditions, almost '…stark naked to the waist with a simple linen petticoat unfastened round it and sometimes turned up as far as the middle of their thighs….' The exuberant Frenchmen named it '*cigarette*' to become the 'the most commonly used French word on the planet', coined by Theophile Gautier, the reputed French poet, writer, art critic and a passionate exponent of French Romanticism. Thus, as a tobacco historian remarked, the 'bastardly offspring of the cigar' was born to seduce the world. The Frenchmen were quick to pick up the cigarette habit and by the middle of nineteenth century, 'suddenly..... it became a *la grande mode* with certain French ladies.' As cigarette smoking progressed to become a common Parisian habit, the French monopoly company SEITA also started producing cigarettes in 1845, and in the first year of its production, sold six million cigarettes.

The Englishmen got the taste of the new smoking fashion through, again, a war: the Crimean War (1853–1856). During the campaign in Crimea, the British troops 'became familiar with the insidious novelty', out of necessity. The pipes were easily broken or unmanageable in battle fields, while cigars were either costly or unobtainable. The Turkish and French allies of the British were already having a 'crude kind of fairly long cigarette or they knew how to roll their own out of crushed tobacco and paper.' On the enemy side, the Russians were also smoking cigarettes made of Turkish or Moroccan tobacco. This novel smoking device was at that time a rarity in England, except the 'poor' or homeless who would roll discarded cigar butts or pipe tobacco into small muskets. When the Crimean War ended, the British troops 'brought home with them a new form of nourishing an old habit'. These warriors were the 'darling of the day'. They smoked the cigarettes gaily as an 'art learned in mysterious East'. And suddenly, 'cigarettes had a flash of popularity with clubmen and others' in England. Both France and England adopted the new smoking fashion 'for its novelty and because it set users apart from the more common smokers of cigars and pipe'.

On the other side of the Atlantic, American travellers returning from England introduced the cigarette 'as a delectable curiosity especially suitable for the elite'. Initially, most of the British, French and later on, Americans, considered the cigarette to be a silly novelty, a trivial fad, designed for the dandies and snobs and would soon pass out. But 'a new cycle of smoking fashion' had quietly begun. Then there came the American Civil War (1861–1865), and 'cigarettes seemed so tailor-made that they might have been designed by a quartermaster.' They were easier to carry than other tobacco products, taking up less room in a man's pack than cigars, and weighing less than a pipe and a pouch of blend. 'A fellow might long for a leisurely smoke, but there was seldom time; an exchange of gunfire, a few minutes of puffing, and another exchange of gun-fire – this was the pattern of the soldier's days, and while most men just stuck with their cigars, sometimes lighting the same one several times, keeping it in their mouths, both lit and unlit for hours at stretch, other men were stoking themselves with cigarettes.' Moreover, it turned out to be a 'better tonic'. The cigarettes made of Virginia tobacco had a higher percentage of nicotine content, compared to the cigar or pipe tobacco, which provided 'a kick', even though it tasted milder than other tobacco products. That was 'exactly what a soldier needed to fortify himself as his fellow warriors dropped from bullets or disease and he wondered whether he would be next.'

When the Civil War ended, the soldiers of the up-and-coming nation went back to their cigars or pipes, considering the cigarettes as 'effeminate little doods'. Curiously enough, during the pre-civil war period as well as after the end of the fighting, American women were found to be indulging themselves in smoking cigarettes in a manner, as an observer in New York remarked, '...some of the ladies of this refined and fashion forming metropolis are aping the silly ways of some pseudo-accomplished foreigners in smoking through a weaker and more feminine article which has been most delicately denominated cigarette.'

Meanwhile, two momentous developments had occurred. In 1827, a Stockton-on-Tees based chemist, John Walker invented the 'friction match', as if to assist the smokers, and smoking soon became a 'mobile habit'. Then in 1839, one of the most abnormal developments happened in agriculture the world over. A farm in Caswell County, North Carolina was producing a lighter coloured tobacco known as 'Piedmont'. A young and intelligent black headman of the Caswell planter, Stephen, while watching the curing of a crop of tobacco fell asleep due the warmth of the wood fires in the barn. Suddenly, he woke up to find that the fires were nearly out. Stephen, in a panic, rushed to a nearby charcoal pit, got hold of some charred logs and piled them up on the dying embers. And then something unique happened, the sudden drying heat derived from the charred logs' turned the leaves into the colour of gold. The golden variety of tobacco was easiest to inhale, without intoxicating the smoker. It was a significant discovery.

After the civil war, a 'peace meeting' was arranged at Durham's Station, North Carolina, in 1865. While the generals of both sides were engaged with 'peace terms', the soldiers had the opportunity to savour the flavour of the new 'golden' tobacco. They were enthralled and became instant converts to cigarettes. Soon enough, there was a clamour for this 'wonderful new tobacco' and cigarettes thereby became a tempting smoke for the Americans. Thus, the 'feminine' cigarette, a soldier's favourite in the battle-field and a woman's 'thrill of tasting forbidden fruit' clearly overwhelmed the American smokers. By 1875, Americans smoked forty-two million cigarettes and the figure rose to 500 million by 1880. In 1883, the *New York Times* warned: 'The decadence of Spain began when Spaniards adopted cigarettes and if this pernicious practice obtains among adult Americans the ruin of the Republic is close at hand.'

It was a period of phenomenal growth for cigarette smoking in the United States, particularly and vigorously promoted by Allen and Ginter under the brand name of Bull Durham. People were longing for more, but the supply was falling short of the enormity of the demand. These

A Bull Durham mural in Collinsville, Illinois.

'little white tobacco cylinders' were still being rolled by hand and it was simply impossible to roll out enough quantity to meet the growing demand. Realising the problem, Allen and Ginter offered a prize of $75,000 to anyone who could invent a cigarette making machine. James Albert Bonsack, the twenty-one-year old son of a plantation owner, and something of a tinkerer by profession, took up the challenge and created a rather strange looking device 'consisting of belts, pulleys, nuts and bolts, gears and gizmos' which would automatically roll out up to 212 cigarettes per minute.

Bonsack got the device patented in his name and presented it to Allen and Ginter. The trial run was indeed faulty. 'It seldom managed to function at its optimum rating.' Allen and Ginter rejected the machine; perhaps because they did not want to pay the prize money or they were 'simply frightened of machines'. However, James 'Buck' Duke, the young head of a small Virginian tobacco company, foresaw the potential of this 'strange' device and installed two Bonsacks in his tobacco factory. He 'brought in a mechanic to do a little fine-tuning', and on 30 April 1884, history was created. The machine ran for full ten hours turning out 120,000 cigarettes. That was the REVOLUTION: the modern cigarette was born on that day. 'Within five years of installing his two Bonsack machines, Duke was selling two million cigarettes a day, more every week than the French smoked in a year, and was making profits other manufacturers could only dream of.' This ensued a flurry among the cigarette manufacturers to obtain the Bonsack machine, including the Bristol-based British giant WD & HO Wills.

As the nineteenth century was drawing to an end, most of the cigarette manufacturers mechanised their operations and 'Buck' Duke, the one-time owner of a small scale tobacco company turned cigarette baron, founded American Tobacco Company in 1889, with an eye to lord over not only the domestic market, but also to capture the up-and–coming market across the Atlantic. Duke's prime target was the smoke-happy English market. He sailed across the Atlantic with great pomp and a show of wealth, threatening to buy over English tobacco companies. Faced with this threat, thirteen 'family-run' English companies met together in December 1901, and formed the Imperial Tobaccos with Sir William Wills as president. There followed a war of wits for market supremacy between the two rivals, and finally a compromise was reached and the British American Tobacco (BAT) was created in 1902 to rule over the 'world of smoke'.

Around the first decade of the twentieth century, the cigarette had reached almost every nook and corner of the globe, except the polar region. Cigarette factories were set

An advertisement for Ryukyu Tobacco published in a Japanese magazine The Okinawa Graphic, *February 1961.*

up all over the world, including off-beat places like India, Ceylon, Egypt, Holland, Belgium, Indonesia, East Africa and Malaya. Some national level tobacco establishments like Japan Tobacco International (1898), Imperial Tobacco Company of India (1910), Tobacco Australia (1913), and China National Tobacco Corporation (1982), also played a stellar role in controlling and promoting the 'smoke' industry in the respective areas of their operation.

The phenomenal growth of cigarette smoking in the twentieth century was largely influenced by three unique factors: war, advertising and the movie. With two cataclysmic world wars, regional conflicts or skirmishes, and even revolutions, and social, political and economic upheavals in various parts of the world, the twentieth century was the bloodiest century of warfare in human history. And, all

Philip Morris Cigarettes, Johnny on the Spot, 1938.

clashes of arms or struggles generated, for obvious reasons, a heavy demand for cigarettes for the fighting men-at-arms. Cigarette was a 'must' item of soldiers' ration, and even the Red Cross volunteers and nurses carried packs of cigarettes for the wounded and helped the disabled men to light their favourite fag. To the soldiers, 'cigarettes were more than mild anaesthetics. Cigarettes formed an umbilical cord linking soldier to civilization. There were little else in the daily grind of being bombed, burned and maimed, of killing or being killed in foreign countries to remind them of home.'

The bloody battles were a boom time for the tobacco bandwagons. American cigarette manufacturers were quick to cash in on America's involvement in the World Wars.

Cigarettes being presented to some of the wounded officers at Kitchener Hospital, Brighton, 1915.

They advertised slogans like: 'America's best for America's bravest', 'Smoke out the Kaiser', or 'when our boys light up the Huns will light out'. Chesterfield, a popular brand was promoted as: 'Keep 'em smoking, our fighting men Rate the Best'. The brand Camel declared: 'Camels are the favourite! In the Army…. In the Navy….In the Marine Corps…In the Coast Guard!' and 'You Want Steady Nerves When You're Flying Uncle Sam's Bombers Across the Ocean.' The 'Lucky Strike' announced, 'Lucky Strike Green has gone to war.'

Advertising, a major factor for the growth of cigarette consumption, was in essence a by-product of the tobacco industry. It all began, rather humbly, about a couple of centuries ago when tobacco became an important commercial product in its own right. The tobacco products were then promoted by using 'Indian images' because of the weed's 'gift of god' tag with respect to the American natives. Famous native figures of Uncas, Red Cloud, Black Hawk, Pocahontas, Wenonah etc., or the titles like Great Chief, Indian Princes, and Grand Sachem, with accompanying scenes of hunting or making war, were widely publicised through the then visual media. All the figures, even the females, were armed, implying association of strength, power and aggressiveness, which were carried over into the twentieth century as tobacco's connection with 'manliness' or 'individualism'.

Toward the end of the nineteenth century and in early twentieth century, with the mechanised mass production of cigarettes, there ensued a mad rush among the cigarette manufacturers for a larger market share. Initially, some of the American companies enticed the consumers by distributing

*An Army Girl's Transport Tobacco Fund advertisement
during the Great War.*

coupons with each packet, offering attractive gifts like sets
of university pennants, blankets, maps on silk, lithographed
books of architecture and other educational trivia. Later on,
pictorial cards were inserted into each packet, displaying
busts of prima donnas…sporting girls solidly encased in
tights…bathing beauties wearing suits only to their knees,
gladiators, heroes of the baseball field, etc. The British
manufacturers on the other hand maintained a sober
approach. Their promotional cards portrayed royalty or
displayed ships and the likes. The scheme was quite popular
in the Continent as well, particularly in France, Belgium

*Anglo-Indian actress, Merle Oberon on the cover on
a cigarette pack, 1940.*

and Germany, and found its way as far as China and the Far
East. These novel cigarette cards would go on to becoming
a collectors' delight.

The twentieth century brought about a change in the
smoking fashion, as well as 'advertising became more insistent,

A sketch for Sunflower cigarettes by Leo Gestel.

more intrusive and more of an accepted concomitant of the commercial world.' Several fascinating brands surfaced in the market with moisture-proof and non-combustible paper, built-in striker at the lighting end, filter tip, cigarettes made of roasted tobacco, and chemically treated with menthol, targeting the 'youth market', as well as the 'feminine members of the society', the 'decent, respectable women' in particular, proclaiming 'empowerment' or 'freedom' for them. In 1924, the British tobacco firm, Philip Morris, which had since shifted its base to New York, came out with a brand for women called 'Marlboro' with a slogan 'Mild as May', especially 'engineered for women, incorporating an ivory tip of greaseproof paper to prevent them adhering to lipstick.' The advertising campaign for this special brand was initiated rather cautiously with a query: 'Has smoking any more to do with woman's morals than has the colour of her hair?' Marlboro was a big hit with fashionable women, shuttling in limousines, or attending bridge parties. James Bull, a Milwaukee firm introduced 'cocarettes', 'a soothing blend of refreshing Colombian cocoaleaf and lightest Virginian tobacco, specially blended for the Lady's need.'

Edward Bernays, the father of modern day 'Public Relations', staged a burlesque show for his client, the American Tobacco Company, to break the social taboo against women smoking cigarettes. 'He hired a group of women to dress as suffragettes, and march in formation in a parade down Fifth Avenue in New York city on Easter Sunday, 1929. When they reached the section of elevated seats reserved for the press, the faux suffragettes all pull out cigarettes, lit them up, and proclaimed them to be *freedom*

*The 1929 'Torches of Freedom' public relations campaign equated
smoking with female emancipation. This image from Germany
actually predates the American campaign. In various forms and
places around the world, the campaign continues to this day.*

torches.' The later-day iconic cigarette advertisements,
'you've come a long way baby', aimed at women, were but
the echo of Bernays' bizarre road-show, associating smoking
with women's rights. The prospective young smokers were
enticed with slogans like: 'Have a Camel' or 'Camels never
tire the taste', or 'Reach for a Lucky, instead of a sweet',
later on modified to 'fat is bad and can be kept at bay by
smoking', and the like. In smoke-heaven England, John
Player of the Castle Tobacco Factory, Nottingham, came out
with catchy brand names like Our Heroes, Our Charming
Belles, The Castle, and so on. The cigarette manufacturers
were spending astronomical sums on advertising through
print and electronic media, leaving no stone unturned
to 'push' their products, making cigarette 'an irresistible
enticement for most of the mankind'.

And, then came the Movie. It drastically changed the concept, as well as the fashion of smoking. The 'habit' adopted centuries ago by the 'civilised' world from the Mayans, the Aztecs, or the North American Natives, reached its zenith of popularity. The Freudian concept of 'lip eroticism', associated with smoking, was at the height of its sensuous glory when the 'talking' and 'singing' movie idols 'effectively knocked out the need to justify smoking'. The cigarettes, pipes or cigars smoked by the movie heroes appeared gigantic on the silver screen, in front of millions of viewers around the world, making smoking 'as natural as eating or kissing'. People not only idolised their heroes, they were slavishly imitated. '…the best way of impersonating a hero or heroine was via their smoking habit. People began to smoke because their favourite film stars did. The cheapness and availability of cigarettes were to their advantage.' The cigarette's role as 'a lover's go-between' on the silver screen or 'a substitute for a kiss or more' captured the imagination of audience the world over. Just as once tobacco served as 'money' in the past, 'it now acted as the international currency of desire.'

By middle of the twentieth century, Count Corti, a tobacco historian observed 'a glance at the statistics proves convincingly that non-smokers are a feeble and dwindling minority…all countries, whatever their form of government, now encourage and facilitate the passion of smoking in every conceivable way, merely for the sake of revenue which it produces….' As the accursed century was coming to a close, whether rich or poor, famous or obscure, cigarettes, as observed by tobacco historian, Iain Gatley, were found to be the 'most democratic commodity in common use'.

And, a massive 1.5 to 1.9 billion people the world over are expected to be smoking by the year 2025, as estimated by the World Health Organisation.

The Fate

SOMETIME IN 1809, or a little earlier, Louis Nicolas Vauquelin, a French Chemist, discovered the active principle in tobacco and named it 'Nicotianine', after Jean Nicot. He was, however, not able to isolate it completely. It was left to the follow-up researchers, L Posselt and F A Reimann, who, in 1828, successfully separated the 'ingredient' that came to be known the world over as the infamous 'nicotine'. It was the nicotine component which set tobacco apart from other plants. This 'active ingredient' of tobacco was 'volatile, colourless, oily liquid, and a poisonous alkaloid'. The essential oil of tobacco was considered to be a 'most potent poison', and an internal dose of sixty milligram was supposed to be enough to kill a man of normal health. Soon thereafter, tobacco earned the notoriety as an 'agent of murder'.

The first warning bell about the health hazard of tobacco was sounded 5,000 years ago, when *Ayurveda*, the ancient Indian science of medicine, while identifying the 'weed' as medicinal herb, a cure for many common human ailments, also cautioned that excessive, improper or oddly timed use of *tamrakuttah* or *tamakhu,* aka tobacco 'develops drunkenness, bile and giddiness. Sometimes, vomiting....

Constant use of tobacco diminishes the strength of eye-sight and makes semen virile and more burning.' However, the most ancient instance of tobacco related afflictions could not be traced within the scope of this present work, except that some of the tobacco shamans in their quest for achieving the 'altered states of consciousness' succumbed to death, due to overdose of tobacco juice or excessive smoking.

Girolami Benzoni, an Italian, was one of the first Europeans to record his displeasure about tobacco in writing. The Italian visited the 'New World' in 1541 and wrote down his experience: 'See what a wicked and pestiferous poison from the devil this must be! It happened several times to me that, going through the provinces of Guatemala and Nicaragua, I have entered the house of an Indian who hath taken this herb, which in Mexican language is called *Tabaco*, and immediately perceiving the sharp, fetid smell, I was obliged to go away and seek some other place.' Some Indians took so much tobacco that Benzoni claimed, 'that they fall down as if they were dead and remain the greater part of the day and night unconscious.'

In about 1583, Pope Sixtus ordained: 'Under pain of mortal sin, no priest, before celebrating and administering the Communion, should take tobacco in smoke or powder, not even for medical reasons.' His successor, Urban VIII, banned the use of tobacco in any form in 1624 across all Catholic churches, complaining: 'the use of the herb commonly called tobacco has gained so strong a hold on persons of both sexes, yea, even priests and clerics.' The succeeding Papal heads through the greater part of the seventeenth century, maintained a similar attitude towards this 'new world' fancy, though, the Papal ban was partially relaxed by Pope Benedict XIII in about 1669.

Towards the end of sixteenth century, when Elizabethan England took to smoking, rather with a vengeance, there was a rumbling of discontent among a section of the English society about this 'obnoxious' habit. The latent feeling was given vent to in a satirical opus: *Worke for Chimney Sweepers*, penned by an unknown English writer under the pseudonym of Philaretes, in 1602, just a year before the death of Queen Elizabeth. The opus 'claimed that the leaf would make the brain so sooty that an entire army of the title characters would be required to cleanse it.' But the 'most famous anti-smoking tract of the era' came in 1604 from King James I: *A Counterblaste to Tobacco*. The publication of the pamphlet, according to some accounts, was inspired by the King's hatred towards the flamboyant favourite of the late Queen, Sir Walter Raleigh. Whatever might have been the reason, the obsessive King James 'hated tobacco and was an active tobacco hater', and publicly condemned the indulgence in 'precious stink'. He wrote unabashedly in the pamphlet: '(why do we) abase ourselves so farre as to imitate those beastly Indians, slaves to the Spaniards, refuse to the world, and as yet aliens to the holy Convent of the God? Why do we not as well imitate them in walking naked as they doe? ... Yea, why do we not denie God and adore the Devill as they doe?' The King concluded his rhetoric 'in a note of fine frenzy', 'A custom loathsome to the eye, hateful to the nose, harmful to the brain, dangerous to the lungs, and in the black stinking fume thereof, nearest resembling the horrible Stygian smoke of the pit that is bottomless.'

King James intent on banning tobacco, but his advisers insisted that it would be almost impossible to implement the ban for many obvious reasons, and was certainly not going to be cost–effective. A reluctant King resorted to an alternative measure to curb the 'precious stink', taxation. He raised the quantum of tax from the existing two pence per pound of tobacco to six shillings and ten pence, an increase of 4,000 per cent in one go. He also forced a 'special fee for a licence' on the tobacco tradesmen and the manufacturers of tobacco pipes, to the delight of the smugglers and displeasure of honest traders.

The first half of the seventeenth century was indeed a period of turbulence in tobacco history, an era of horrid experiences for the first generation tobacco users. While tobacco saved England's Jamestown colony in the 'new world', and was trying to gain a foot-hold in the 'old world' Europe and elsewhere in the globe as a medicinal herb or a 'pleasure' habit or both, it had to face considerable opposition from the then monarchs and despots of the period. Close on the heels of King James' *Counterblaste*, many European countries imposed prohibitive orders against the consumption as well as cultivation of tobacco. Apart from the 'stink' factor, their main concern was about the progressive diversion of agricultural land towards the cultivation of tobacco, a cash crop, at the cost of food grain production. Laws were passed in Sweden, Denmark, Russia, Naples, Sicily, Papal States, Electorate of Cologne, Wurttemberg, Austria, Hungary and Germany, where smoking in particular was 'perceived in statute as only little more commendable than adultery, and the two were treated in a similar manner.' Punishments included fines, confiscation of properties, disfigurement, and even death.

In Russia, Michael Feodorovich, the first Romanov Tsar (1613–45), declared consumption of tobacco a 'capital offence' and set up a 'tobacco court' to try the law breakers, penalising the offenders with slitting of lips, or flogging, often fatally with a 'knout' (multiple leather thongs with metal wires or hooks attached to it). Sometimes, offenders were castigated or exiled to Siberia, stripping them of all their properties. It was indeed a devilish treatment to the tobacco offenders about which F.W. Fairholt, a tobacco historian recorded: 'Was ever the destruction of body and spirit threatened so unjustly? Mutilation for just taking a pinch! Loss of life for lighting a pipe! Exclusion from heaven or perhaps harmlessly reviving attention to a wearisome sermon in a chapel or church! Merciful heaven! What commination these to emanate from Christian Kings and Christ's successors!'

It was an even more harrowing tale in the Islamic world. The Islamic despots of the period 'deemed smoking a despicable social habit', and since Koran did not permit it, 'it must be forbidden'. Shah Abbas (1571–1629), the first Safavid King of Iran, was the earliest among the Islamic rulers to discourage public consumption of tobacco. He was, however, not harsh enough to enforce his diktats against tobacco users, but later on, his own grandson behaved barbarically, once commanding a minion to pour molten lead down the throats of two people who smoked in public. Turkey, 'the land that would one day rank among world's leading growers and exporters of leaf, its name synonymous with smoother blends and richest tastes', had experienced an agonising time as an anonymous traveller recorded: 'an unfortunate Turk conducted about the streets of Constantinople in 1610, mounted backwards on an ass with tobacco pipe driven through the cartilage of his nose, for the crime of smoking.' In 1633, Murad IV, historically infamous as 'Murad the Cruel', declared tobacco a capital offence in Turkey. He had despised smoking ever since a firework display celebrating the birth of his first son had burned down half of his capital, Constantinople. Murad adopted a ubiquitous method to trace the 'tobacco offenders'. He would wander through Constantinople in disguise, of various sorts, ask those whom he encountered for some leaf, and ordered those who complied to be beheaded. According to contemporary records, in this process, Murad had beheaded more than 25,000 suspected Turkish smokers within a period of about fourteen years.

Tobacco ran into trouble in the Far East too. Japan's rulers who were initially hostile to 'foreign influences', banned the 'alien origin' weed in 1609, 1612, 1615 and 1616, each time with increasingly severe penalties that included fines, imprisonment and confiscation of properties. In 1640, the last Ming emperor of China announced death sentences for the smokers. In India, the fourth Mughal Emperor Jahangir reportedly 'decreed that smokers have their lips slit so that a pipe would never again rest comfortably between them.'

As the seventeenth century was coming to a close, most of the dreaded orders about tobacco were either rescinded or allowed to lapse. It was not only the outcome of 'persistent

appetites' of tobacco users, but an 'irresistible' force of the
'economic and fiscal importance of tobacco'. The monarchs
and despots, 'with all their powers and savagery', realised
that they needed 'revenue resources to sustain colonies…to
create a powerful navy and develop world trade' to survive
in an era of 'dramatic and turbulent' happenings all around
them. With the introduction of state monopolies, licensing
systems and taxation, tobacco turned into a horn of plenty.
It became too powerful a fiscal instrument to fill up the
Treasury. 'The brown leaves of tobacco had acquired a glitter
indistinguishable from gold. Various laws and regulations
against smoking remained on books and were conveniently
forgotten.' All the silly arguments about 'morality' or 'public
health' were blown over, and people were merrily smoking
or chewing or sniffing tobacco with no fear of public
prosecution.

On the other side of the Atlantic, in the 'new world'
colonies, there were some feeble attempts to curb the
tobacco habit. Laws restricting public smoking were passed
in Connecticut, New Haven, Massachusetts and Plymouth.
New Haven imposed a fine of eighty-four pence for each
case of transgression; while Massachusetts declared tobacco
a 'solitary pleasure' and decreed 'people were no longer to
smoke in groups'. Plymouth village authorities forbade the
consumption of tobacco within a mile of a dwelling and
outlawed it completely in firm fields and rooms at inns. In
New Amsterdam (later to be known as New York), its Dutch
Director-General, William Keift, banned the use of tobacco
altogether. The ban was, later on, lifted under the pressure
of the world's 'first smoke-in' agitation. All the anti-tobacco

laws were in the end dramatically defused, with the birth of the United States of America, as the new and expanding nation 'seemed to require the expanded use of tobacco as a condition of its growth'.

In 1798, Benjamin Rush, the famed physician, one of the founding fathers of the United States of America and a signatory to the Declaration of Independence, came out with an essay: *Observations upon the influence of Habitual use of Tobacco upon Health, Morals and Property*. It was the first positive reaction about the effect of 'Demon Tobacco', coming from the land that had ironically gifted the 'Demon Tobacco' to the modern day world. Rush pointed out 'that the weed was particularly harmful to the mouth, stomach, and nerves', and insisted that 'smoking and chewing provoked drunkenness'. He strongly opposed smoking of pipes and cigars. His observations were the unofficial start of American anti-smoking movement.

In the wake of Rush's comments, a group of noted United States educators, some members of the clergy and a few physicians launched a steady and solemn attack on the use of tobacco. Horace Greeley, the legendary journalist of the time and the founder editor of *New York Tribune*, characterised the cigar as 'a fire at one end and a fool at the other'. Dr Joel Shew (1816-1855) in his book: *Tobacco Diseases: with a remedy for the habit*, traced 'delirium tremens, perverted sexuality, impotency, insanity, and cancer to the effects of smoking and chewing.' The unofficial campaign against tobacco in the U S initially 'ranged from temperate advice to passionate denunciation', but with the advent of Civil War (1861-1865), all the persuasions or rational advice faded away as no one, on either side, was interested in depriving the soldiers of their 'essential comfort habit'.

After the Civil War, America witnessed a conspicuous rise in the consumption of tobacco, particularly smoking of cigarettes. Bonsack's automatic cigarette rolling machine and affordability of cigarettes were the main contributing factors in this surge for smoking. The defused pre-Civil War anti-tobacco campaign, however, got a fresh lease of life with the emergence of a 'bony' and 'masculine' lady: Lucy Page Gaston (1860-1924), an ardent anti-tobacco crusader. Initially, Gaston along with her mother was involved in the 'abolition and temperance movement' and had joined the Woman's Christian Temperance Union (WCTU) as an active member. Initially, she did not pay much attention to tobacco and dismissed it 'as more of a ghastly habit than a pressing issue'. But Gaston joined the anti-tobacco movement when WCTU's Health and Hygiene Wing, looking into the effects of smoking, observed that 'tobacco was a problem in its own right because it led to alcohol, which, in turn, leads to the devil'. The WCTU findings further recorded: 'as liquor impaired the moral sense, so nicotine impaired the capacity to love and thus contributed to broken marriages. Nicotine could also inflict instantaneous physical injury.' The report cited the case of a boy whose face had been completely disfigured after he had smoked a few cigarettes, and of another, a fourteen-year-old, who dropped dead immediately after his first cigarette. And, as a journalist recounted, Gaston 'saw the anti-cigarette front relatively unguarded … and made for it pell-mell.'

In 1899, Gaston founded the Chicago Anti-Tobacco League, the first group of its kind in the United States. That was a time when 'tobacco was in the air, and like the even more pungent scent of Chicago's slaughter houses, people took it as a sign of good times and economic well-being.' Gaston had a tough time explaining or demonstrating the harmful effects of smoking on the human body and mind. Yet, through lectures and mailings and occasional newspaper articles, her message was conveyed widely enough. Within a period of two years of the inception of the League, she was able to expand it into the Anti-Cigarette League of America, claiming a membership of 300,000 people across the USA and Canada. She also published a magazine called *The Boy,* which advised America's youth on how to avoid the temptations of cigarette smoking, and even if they did succumb, then how to cure themselves of the consequences. She also at times resorted to 'guerrilla tactics' to fight the menace. She would instruct the children to find adults who were smoking in public and sneak up behind them. When the adults seemed to be looking elsewhere or were not paying attention for some reason or the other, the kids were to snatch the cigarettes from their mouths and run away as fast as they could. She pleaded with the merchants not to hire boys and girls who smoked, or if they did, to insist that the youngsters sign pledges to give up the weed as a condition of employment. Some of the business houses complied with her request and even extended monetary support to her cause. Gaston also demanded that the Chicago civic authorities 'appoint special anti-cigarette policemen who would not only arrest the offenders but lecture them on the spot about the self-destructiveness of their ways.'

Statistically, it could not be ascertained how effective Gaston's battle against smoking was, but she was able to elicit 'moral support' from some of the notable personalities of the period. Elbert Hubbard, a celebrated humourist wrote: 'Cigarette smokers are men whose future lies behind them.' David Starr Jordan, the president of the Stanford University, said: 'Boys who smoked cigarettes are like wormy apples that fall from the tree before they are ripe.' William Booth, the founder of the Salvation Army listing 'fifty four objections of tobacco' pointed out that it 'arrests the growth of the young'. Henry Ford, the celebrated car manufacturer, published a pamphlet: *The case against the Little White Slaver*, addressed to 'My friend, the American boy', endorsing Gaston's views that 'cigarettes were a curse to civilization'. He further asserted that he 'was convinced (that they) contained the vilest poison known to man.' Thomas Edison, the renowned scientist who 'tamed and sold electricity', though himself a compulsive tobacco chewer, was an articulate hater of smoking. According to him 'cigarettes were uniquely dangerous among tobacco products, on account of the paper wrapper which had a violent action on the nerve centres, producing degeneration of the cells of the brain.' Edison was so convinced about the danger of cigarettes that he refused to employ cigarette smokers. The most outspoken comment, however, came from John L Sullivan, the then heavyweight boxing champion of the world. Asked by a reporter about cigarette smoking, he retorted: 'Smoke cigarette? Not on your tut-tut…. You can't

suck coffin-nails and be a ring champion … who smokes
'em? Dudes and college stiffs-fellow who'd be wiped out by
a single jab or a quick uppercut.'

Between 1895 and 1909, twenty-one American states
and territories outlawed cigarettes for children, and twelve
states made them illegal for adults. The defaulters were fined
or jailed, but under 'high-pressure' lobbying by the emerging
cigarette barons, hardly any noticeable action was taken to
enforce the anti-smoking laws. In Chicago, Gaston's own
fort, an alderman was offered 25,000 dollars to vote against
an anti-smoking ordinance. In Tennessee, legislators were
offered 500 dollars to each of them who 'would turn his
back on the reformers' pleas'. The Americans, as yet, could
not scientifically prove that smoking was dangerous by co-
relating the cause and effect syndrome, though some of the
physicians came out with 'smoking cures' like 'mouth wash'
and the likes. The reformers advised people to chew 'gentian
root', whenever they felt the craving for the weed, and to get
plenty of exercise and rest. Despite Gaston's valiant efforts,
most of the people perceived the Anti-Cigarette League of
America 'as a relatively benign group, belonging to mothers,
grandmothers and admirable peoples who paid their taxes
on time and attended civic functions.'

During the Spanish-American War, the US Federal
Government raised the taxes on the weed to finance the
war and was indirectly encouraging people to smoke,
apparently, in connivance with the cigarette manufacturers.
Gaston furiously objected to this unholy tactic. Later on,
when America became involved in the First World War, and
President Woodrow Wilson was found openly supporting

the 'smoke for Soldiers' Fund', Gaston kept on harping, in her characteristic way, about the destructive effects of cigarettes. However, people thought that she was going too far in condemning the wartime use of cigarettes. The gallant crusader, a sprinter and a somewhat disheartened Lucy Page Gaston breathed her last, in August 1924, rather unsung, curiously enough due to throat cancer. By that year, Eric Burns wites: Americans were smoking 'seventy three billion cigarettes, which worked out to 600 for every man, woman and child, and was eighteen times as many small smokes as they had consumed a quarter of a century earlier, when Gaston founded the Chicago Anti-Smoking Cigarette League.'

***

In 1631, the French Parliament banned the consumption of tobacco in all forms for prisoners, when prison doctors reported that the inmates were among the least healthy persons in the land and tobacco seemed to be the cause. It was a case of 'suspicion' only, but it was the first ban of its kind in Europe, on consumption of tobacco products. Since then, for over three hundred years, physicians, scientists and reformers all over the world have been experimenting, researching or debating over the effects of tobacco on the human body and mind.

In 1665, The Royal Society of London experimented with a cat by injecting a few drops of distilled oil of tobacco. The cat dropped dead almost instantly. In 1671, Italian biologist Francesco Redi published an 'account of the lethal effects of the oil of tobacco', but he was basically 'opining more than proving'. By the middle of eighteenth century, the Medical School of Paris declared that using of weed shortened a person's life. But the School did not provide any supportive details to substantiate this observation. The early nineteenth century witnessed the landmark discovery of the lethal 'active ingredient' of tobacco called 'nicotine', as had been mentioned at the beginning of this chapter. With this discovery, advanced medical systems and chemical analysis, tobacco's role as a threat to human metabolism became a subject of a deeper probe for the researchers on the subject.

In 1857, *Lancet*, the British medical journal, based on chemical research, reported that 'the leaf slowed the workings of the mind by producing drowsiness and rendered the mind less efficient by creating irritability.' The journal further went on to claim that 'tobacco caused damage to the respiratory system, as well to the larynx, trachea and bronchae.' Two years later, a French doctor, Bouisson, after examining sixty-eight patients in a hospital in Montpelier, found out that they were suffering from cancer of the mouth, tonsils, or lip and all of them were smokers. In 1889, two English scientists, Langley and Dickinson, published a landmark study on the effect of nicotine on ganglia. They hypothesised 'that the nervous system was comprised of receptors and transmitters that responded stimulation of specific chemicals, one of which was nicotine, which could therefore influence or interfere with the working of the nervous system.' Round-about the same time, eminent newspapers and magazines the world over, including the *New York Times*, prominently carried research-based articles and stories about the disastrous effects of nicotine upon human system.

In 1895, in Wurzburg, Germany, Wilhelm Von Rontgen, discovered the X-ray, revolutionising medical science. The doctors could now 'peer inside living bodies, and to learn the secrets of their bones and lungs.' Knowledge of what smoking might do to its addicts, and how to look for it, was being acquired piece by piece. The evidence discovered thereby was, indeed, alarming. Luther Burbank, the pioneer American botanical geneticist observed that 'cigarettes were nothing more or less a slow but sure form of lingering suicide'.

The debate, however, still lingered on. There was an 'unsolved alchemy' concerning the effects of tobacco on the human body that made the tobacco plant 'more desirable as a source of desirable fume than any other'. It was perhaps not the nicotine content alone that was responsible for the habit forming property of tobacco. There were other ingredients, additional to nicotine, in manufactured tobacco, like nitrogenous and other substances, tars and tobacco oil which produced irritants.

Throughout the 1920s and 1930s, as the habit of smoking thrived, so also there were a number of surveys and reports about tobacco which emerged gradually. In 1921, Dr Moses Barron of the University of Minnesota, after examining the autopsy records from 1899 to 1919, discovered four cases of lung cancer. Just after a period of twelve months, he found out eight more cases. Dr Barron suspected that since more people were smoking, tobacco was responsible for the increased incidence of lung cancer within such a short period. In England, Sir Ernest L Kennaway, a chemist of some standing, published a paper in 1924 on an ingredient in tobacco known as tar. It was a greasy dark, brown or black substance 'produced by the solids in smoke when they settle'. It was this tar, according to him, which caused the cancer. Pierre Schrumpt-Pierron, professor of clinical medicine, University of Cairo, in his book, *Tobacco and Physical Efficiency*, published in 1927, listed out the toxic substances that were produced, besides nicotine, 'from the combustion of the fermented dry leaf.' These were: pyridine, prussic acid, pyrolin, ammonia, collidine and carbon monoxide, out of which the latter two items were considered to be more poisonous than nicotine. Some later analysts added a few more substances to Pierron's list: Carbon dioxide, aldehyde, furfural and alkali. These men of science, however, observed that 'none of the toxic or other substances or their combinations produced normally by the smoking of tobacco (appeared) to have an adverse physiologic effect upon human body.' But it was evident that excessive smoking could be dangerous.

In 1929, the doctors Alton Ochsner and Michael De Bakey of the United States, and some scientists of Cologne, Germany, came out with reports of 'strongest statistical correlation yet between smoking and cancer'. They claimed that they studied too many cases and found too many links. In 1938, Dr Raymond Pearl of John Hopkins University, reporting to the New York Academy of Medicine on 'The Search for Longevity', commented that 'smoking is associated with definite impairment of longevity'. The impairment was proportionately 'great for heavy smokers and less for moderate smokers'. In 1939, the German scientist, Franz H Muller, was first to use case-controlled epidemiological methods to document a relationship between smoking and lung cancer. According to him, extraordinary rise in tobacco use was the single most important cause of the rising incidence of lung cancer. Meanwhile, the US Bureau of Census reported that during the period of 1934-38, there was a thirty six per cent increase in death due to lung cancer, which was indeed an alarm bell for the tobacco users, particularly cigarette smokers.

With the outbreak of World War II, a truly global war, the smokers got a booster dosage, muting at least for some time the entire hullabaloo over tobacco's effect on the human body and mind. The soldiers, on either side, with their assured 'ration', or 'donation' of cigarettes, lit their favourite fags at will, while igniting firearms against the enemy posts, almost at every nook and corner of the globe. Cigarettes had enjoyed a quasi-official status during the war period. But those soldiers, who escaped death by enemy gunfire, came back home to encounter a different kind of fire, the side-effects of excessive smoking. The soldiers who had survived one enemy earlier, were now likely to fall victim to a far more insidious enemy.

In 1958, the US Public Health Service after studying 200,000 veterans of World War I and II, came to the conclusion that thirty-two per cent smokers were 'likely to die at an early age than non-smokers', and that heavy smokers were in greater peril than light smokers. This study report was a front page story in the *New York Times*. After the War, scientists and reformers picked up the thread of the anti-tobacco movement, persuasively backed up by big-city newspapers and large-circulation magazines, and critics expressed their views on radio and television explaining the various dangers of the leaf. On 27 May 1950, the *Journal of American Medical Association* published an article written by Morton Levin, an epidemiologist, confirming a statistical link between smoking and lung cancer after surveying smoking habits of 236 cancer patients. In September of the same year, the *British Medical Journal* published a report entitled, 'Smoking and Carcinoma of the Lung', prepared by Richard Doll and A Bradford Hill after studying 1,732 cancer patients and comparing them with 743 non-cancer patients, arriving at the statistics that 'heavy smokers were fifty times as likely as non-smokers to contract lung cancer'. The report concluded that 'smoking is a factor, and an important factor, in the production of carcinoma of the lung.'

In the year 1952, an obscure magazine called the *Christian Herald* published an article based on a rather unusually phrased research project: *Death Watch,* conducted by the American Cancer Society, on the relationship of smoking and lung cancer, drawing public attention to the fact that 800,000 young people every year were risking their lives by becoming addicted to the weed. This article, captioned, *Smokers Are Getting Scared*, was initially noticed by very few people. But it received wider publicity when *Reader's Digest*, arguably the world's most widely read magazine, reprinted the article as *Cancer by the Carton*. The very next year, the *Journal of American Geriatrics* came out with a statement that 'all men who have smoked a package of cigarette a day for twenty years are likely candidates for bronchogenic carcinoma.' This statement also received widest coverage in the United States through print as well as electronic media. Close on the heels of this revelation, in 1954, Drs E Cuyler Hammond and Daniel Horn, both affiliated to the *American Cancer Society*, presented a report, at the annual convention of the *American Medical Association*, based on an exclusive study of 11,780 men between fifty and sixty-nine, all of them smokers, asserting that 'during the period of the study 7,360 of the men died. If all of them had been non-smokers…only 4,651 would have died…. The death of regular cigarette smokers was generally sixty-eight per cent higher than that of the non-smokers, that of smokers of two or more packs a day was 123 per cent higher.' This report, again, received wide media attention throughout the United States.

Meanwhile, Humphry Bogart, the celebrated Hollywood idol and a most conspicuous screen smoker died of lung cancer in 1957. It was heart-breaking news for his numerous fans, as well as for the smokers. The same year, the first ever official awareness campaign about health hazards of smoking was launched in England and the United States, followed by many others in European and other countries in the following years. In England, the Ministry of Health, as advised by the Royal College of Physicians, sent out millions of posters to schools and government offices with a straight forward appeal: 'Before you smoke, think – cigarettes cause cancer.' The television commercials for tobacco were pushed back to late night slots to prevent children from seeing them. In the United States, the Public Health Service availed the services of the print media to forewarn the people about the dangers of frequent use of tobacco as the cause of cancer, citing the results of various studies and reports on the subject.

Alarmed by all these official moves and the rising voice against tobacco, the manufacturers, particularly in the United States, joined their hands together to safeguard their business interests and issued a 'joint pronouncement on the health aspects of smoking' to their valued customers. Their 'Frank Statement to Cigarette Smokers' was placed as an advertisement in 448 newspapers, with a total readership of 43,245,000 people, in 258 cities across America. The 'Frank Statement' dismissed the 'shocking' allegations about cigarette smoking, claiming that it was their genuine interest 'to safeguard public health' and vehemently argued that though the recent medical research indicated tobacco as a 'possible cause of cancer', there was 'no proof that cigarette smoking' was one of the causes. It also pointed out that, statistically, there could be many 'other aspects of modern life' which might cause lung cancer and the 'products' that they were making were not injurious to health. Nonetheless, the scientists and reformers continued their tirade against tobacco manufacturers and lawsuits followed in many US courts, suing tobacco companies for compensation or redress against health hazards. But the defenders of the plaintiffs found it difficult to prove that cigarettes were responsible for the cancer in question against powerful counter arguments placed before the courts by the tobacco tycoons. It was, as yet, beyond the limits of the 'understanding of the causation of cancer' for contemporary medical science. Consequently, plaintiffs continued to die of 'cancer mid-case' or were going 'broke' despite strong reasons to support their cause.

On 7 March 1962, the British Royal College of Physicians published a landmark report entitled: *Smoking and Health*, intended to prove the 'overwhelming case against tobacco'. The report was a big draw for the British public, and editorially commented and debated upon by leading newspapers, including *The Guardian* and *The Times*, on the 'issue of official intervention', giving advice to the people on how to quit smoking. Two years later, on 11 January 1964, the United States Surgeon General, Luther Terry convened a press conference in Washington D C to release a report: *Smoking and Health: Report of the Advisory Committee to the Surgeon General of the Public Health Service*. The comprehensively worded report revealed that there were only '3,000 deaths from lung cancer in United States in 1930, but the figure had climbed to 18,000 in 1950 and to 41,000 in 1962' emphasising the fact that tobacco was culpable to 'other kinds of cancer as well in addition to several non-cancerous ailments.' Based on investigative scientific analysis, the report also listed some of the major tobacco related aliments: oral cancer, cancer of the oesophagus, cancer of the larynx, tobacco amblyopia, peptic ulcer and respiratory ailments.

These two noteworthy reports turned out to mark the turning point in tobacco history, both for tobacco users, particularly cigarette smokers, as well as the tobacco industry, around the world. The tobacco industry furiously reacted to the reports dismissing the findings as merely 'statistics', rather than 'causality'. The cigarette manufacturers in particular counter-attacked the impending government move to curb the smoking habit with considerable pressure, and glamorous publicity through print as well as electronic media, to allure the consumers. People were dazed by the promotional propaganda, compelling the authorities to initiate stern measures to shake the people out of this trance. A series of radical measures followed, during the latter half of the twentieth century.

It all began with labelling the cigarette packets with a statutory warning: 'cigarette smoking may be hazardous to your health', which was later on amended to a direct warning: 'cigarette smoking is dangerous to your health.' This was followed by banning all tobacco advertisements through print and electronic media, as well as on billboards. Posters were sent out to remote areas and TV slots were planted in between prime time programmes with educative messages to avoid tobacco consumption of all sorts. Even more stringent measures followed thereafter. Smokers and non-smokers were initially separated on commercial airlines, followed by a total ban on smoking on all flights. Since 'second-hand smoking' or 'environmental tobacco smoke' was reported to be causing lung cancer and other forms of heart ailments among a large section of people, smoking was progressively receiving a blanket ban in public buildings and private places like workplaces, restaurants, theatres, museums, health or country clubs et al. And lastly, a heavy dosage of taxes was increasingly imposed on all tobacco products, year after year. The resulting effects of all these measures were – if at all someone wanted to indulge themselves in the pleasure of a 'fag', he would have to do so at the cost of dent on the pocket and look for an isolated corner.

The stunned tobacco manufacturers soon came out of their stupor with innovative promotional tactics: by subsidising or sponsoring sporting events, motor racing, athletics meets, cultural events like music or dance festivals, and trade shows or conventions, with a meaningful communication to the TV crew to repeatedly focus on the sponsor's billboards, strategically installed at the venue. However, as the twenty-first century was ushered in, a considerable drop was noticed in smoking habits among the urban educated segment, but it continued to be a rampant habit among the poor working class, semi-literate or illiterate people as an object of 'camaraderie' or a 'simple pleasure' in their otherwise humdrum life style. The Indian

A vintage anti-smoking advertisement, 1905.

sub-continent in particular, experienced a surge in the smoking habit, among the economically underprivileged people, irrespective of age and sex, with easy availability of a low-cost (low taxed, even tax-evasive) hand-made, *tendu (diospyros melanoxylon)* leaf-rolled indigenous smoking device called: *beedi*.

Strangely enough, despite all the warnings and correctional efforts, the lure of tasting the 'forbidden fruit' among the teenagers was rising alarmingly. In the world of cinema, the matinee idols of the young generation were still smoking on the silver screen and some of the rockstar performers earned the notoriety of freely puffing on or off the stage. In imitation of those glamorous screen or stage demigods or goddesses, boys and girls under the age of eighteen were smoking more than before. There is a blanket ban on sale of cigarette and other tobacco products to any one below the age of eighteen in most of the countries, but the mechanism to prevent the clandestine sale or consumption is sadly missing or ineffective.

A survey conducted by the American Cancer Society in 2003 revealed that 'three hundred young people were picking up the cigarette habit *every day*. They were smoking on school grounds even when it was not allowed; they were smoking on sidewalks of town and on the paved plains of shopping malls even when adults looked askance; they were smoking at private parties, where first and second-hand smoke can mingle indiscriminately, working all manners of insidious effects on them.' A very recent survey, conducted by the New York University's Centre for Drug Use and HIV Research, about the behavioural pattern of American school going students, revealed that one in five high school students took to *hookah* smoking. The researchers observed that those students who smoked cigarettes and those who used alcohol or marijuana were more likely to use *hookah*. Behavioural Science researchers attributed this teenage trend to the fact they were 'too young to fathom the limits of mortality' and to the 'pressure of growing up' in today's highly competitive world, in order to 'seek release from the strains' of the struggle for survival.

According to a World Health Organisation, 80,000 to 100,000 children start smoking every day, world-wide, roughly half of whom live in Asia. A very recent WHO report indicates that there are about 246 million smokers and 290 million smokeless tobacco users in South-East Asian region alone. The report further says that one person dies every six seconds due to tobacco related ailments, which works out to about six million deaths globally, annually. If the current trend continues, the figure may touch eight million, by the year 2030.

The Future

STATUTORY WARNINGS APART, cigarette packs now come with almost a full-length display of scary visuals of cancer in many countries, including India. Whether these scary visuals are actually effective in scaring away the habitual or aspiring smokers, is yet to be established.

E-cigarettes, in myriad flavours, are very much in the market as a form of surrogate smoking. This novel electronic smoking device is already under the scanner of the medical researchers and Behavioural Science gurus, scrutinising its role as a Messiah of the 'no tobacco' movement.

Some corporate houses, particularly in the United States of late, have initiated 'financial incentive' schemes for those who quit smoking. The nascent experiment is yet to reach its full maturity as an effective measure for the *future*.

Researchers from the Universities of Granada in Spain and San Buenaventura in Bogota claim that 'Motivational Interviewing' would manage, at least temporarily, the emotional response associated with tobacco, from pleasant to unpleasant, which could help the tobacco users to overcome the main obstacles for quitting tobacco consumption: the motivation for change. We look forward to the *future* to listen to the success stories of 'Motivational Interviewing'.

Psychologists and tobacco-addiction specialists, based on some scientific evidence, think that 'smoking is the killer, not nicotine'. People 'smoke for nicotine but die from tar'. According to them, a daily dose of moderate nicotine 'could be as benign as the caffeine many of us get from a morning cup of coffee'. Nicotine, according to Behavioural Brain Researchers, has the 'potential to prevent Alzheimer's disease, and to delay the onset of Parkinson's in near future.'

Surely, we can wait for the *near future* to know more about the 'potential' benefits of nicotine.

An Israeli scientist, professor Oded Shoseyov of Hebrew University in Jerusalem, reportedly succeeded in producing a replica of the human collagen from the tobacco plant – the main protein in the skin, tendons, bone, cartilage and connective tissues. This tobacco plant-based synthetic collagen could someday be cosmetically used for beauty enhancement, including slowing the onset of wrinkles as one ages, and other medicinal purposes. Good news indeed for the *future*.

Charles Kingsley (1819–1875), a priest of the Church of England, professor, historian and author of many memorable works, including the widely read *The Water Babies* and *Westward HO!*, summed up the weed's virtue as: 'A lone man's companion, a bachelor's friend, a hungry man's food, a sad man's cordial, a wakeful man's sleep, and a chilly man's fire.'

Sir Compton Mackenzie (1883–1972), political activist, a prolific writer of fictions, and the famed author of *Whiskey Galore* and *Sublime Tobacco*, who died a natural death at the age of eighty-nine, recounted his romance with tobacco: 'in the course of my life I have smoked 200,000 pipefuls of tobacco at the very least, and probably nearer quarter of a million. The volume of smoke from these pipes might not disgrace Vesuvius when not in full eruption. My memory is crystal clear. My power of concentration is undiminished. My digestion is perfect. My heart is sound.'

Albert Einstein (1879–1955), decidedly the greatest twentieth century scientist, the developer of the Theory of Relativity, believed 'that pipe smoking contributes to a somewhat calm and objective judgement in all human affairs.'

We might have to wait for another century, a millennium may be, for the *future* Kingsleys, Mackenzies, or Einsteins, to evaluate afresh the esoteric attributes of the mystique weed; and for a *future* Byron to sing in praise, or a *future* Charles Lamb to cry 'farewell' to the 'Gift of Gods'.

Epilogue

THIS IS CERTAINLY not the whole story. Many vital facts and figures and tobacco-related historic events have been inadvertently, or to some extent purposefully left out. But I believe, I have been able to recast the scenario thought-provokingly enough for the valued readers and researchers to dig deeper into the mysteries of the multi-faced seductive weed, for the benefit of posterity. I would like to conclude my story with a few anecdotes, curiously relevant to the extraordinary human-tobacco love affair:

A news item regarding a maiden's wish, picked up from a New York paper:

> 'A thoughtful girl says that when she dies she desires to have tobacco planted over her grave, so that the weed nourished by her dust may be chewed by her bereaved lovers.'

Harvard Medical researchers observed: 'Americans with mental illness are nearly twice likely to smoke cigarettes as people with no mental illness...people with diagnosable mental illness comprised nearly forty-five per cent of the tobacco market in USA, thus implying that almost half of American smokers do so because they are insane.'

A survey jointly undertaken by the Royal College of Physicians and the Royal College of Psychiatrists, UK, reported: 'Smoking may be a sign of psychiatric illness...of the ten million smokers in the UK, up to three million have mental disorders.'

A British official survey reported: 'a smoker can expect to live sixteen years less than a non-smoker, which amounts to an average saving in pension costs, television licence discounts, bus passes and winter fuel allowances of about 250,000 pound sterling per smoker... It would be financial madness for the British government to ban smoking, and unless a better argument than its official estimated death toll of 120,000 smokers per annum can be found, smoking is unlikely to be prohibited in the British Isles.'

Louis-Napoleon III, Emperor of the Second French Empire, when asked to take action against the vice of smoking, remarked: 'This vice brings in one hundred million francs in taxes every year. I will certainly forbid it at once, as soon as you can name a virtue that brings in as much revenue.'

Conversation between General Montgomery and Prime Minister Churchill:

MONTGOMERY: 'I do not drink. I do not smoke. I sleep a great deal. That is why I am 100 per cent fit.'

CHURCHILL: 'I drink a great deal, I sleep little, and

I smoke cigar after cigar. That is why I am 200 per cent fit.'

The president of the Anti-cigarette League of America injected a cat with a hypodermic syringe full of tobacco juice. Result: In a few minutes the cat began to quiver, tremble, and then it had cramps, and in less than twenty minutes, the cat with all its proverbial nine lives, died after violent convulsions.

Larry White, a death row prison inmate in Huntsville, Texas, desired to have a last puff of cigarette before his execution. His request was rejected 'on the grounds that it would have been bad for his health.'

Bibliography

Bain, John Jr—Tobacco in Song and Story. (1896)—Arthur Gray & Co. New York.

Brooks, Jerome E.—Mighty Leaf. (1952)—Little, Brown and Company, Boston.

Burns, Eric—The Smoke of the Gods. (2007)—Temple University Press, Philadelphia.

Conley, Robert J.—The Cherokee Nation—A History. (2005)—University of Mexico Press, Albuquerque.

Deans, Bob—The River Where America Began. (2007)—Rowman & Littlefield Publishers, Inc., Lanham, Maryland.

Elwin, Verrier—The Baiga. (1939)—John Murray, London.
—When The World Was Young. (1961, reprinted 1966)—The Publication Division, Government of India, Delhi.

Gately, Iain—Tobacco: A Cultural History of How an Exotic Plant Seduced Civilization. (2001)—Grove Press, New York. First published by Simon & Schuster U K Ltd., London.

Gore, Al--The Future. (2013)—Random House, New York.

Heizer, R.F. and Whipple M.A.—California Indians-A Source Book. (1951)—University of California Press, Berkley.

Leach, Maria (Ed.)—Standard Dictionary of Folklore, Mythology and Legend Vol. II (1950)—Funk & Wagnalls Company, New York.

Martin, Joel W.—The Land Looks After Us. (1999 reprinted 2001)—Oxford University Press Inc., New York. First printed as: Native American Religion.

Panchamukhi, A.R. – Tobacco in Ancient Indian Literature. Centre for Multi-Disciplinary Development Research, Dharwar, Karnataka, India. CMDR Monograph No: 23.

Pierre, Mark St. & Soldier, Tilda Long-Walking the Sacred Manner—Healers, Dreamers and Pipe carriers: Medicine Women of Plains Indians. (1950)—Touchstone-Rockefeller Centre, New York, Published by Simon & Schuster Inc.

Rafy, (Mrs) K.U.—Folk tales of the Khasis. (1920)—Macmillan, reprinted 2012 by Forgotten Books, London.

Regier, Willis G. (ed.)—Masterpieces of American Indian Literature. (2005)—University of Nebraska Press (Bison Books), Lincoln.

Sharer, Robert J.—Daily Life in Maya Civilization. (2009)—Greenwood Press, London.

Shechter, Relli—Smoking, Culture and Economy in the Middle East. (2006)—I.B. Tauris & Co. Ltd., London.

Smithsonian Institute—Handbook of North American Indians, Vol-IV.—History of Indian-White Relations. (1988)—Smithsonian Institute, Washington D.C.

Taylor, Colin F. (ed.)—Native American Myths and Legends. (1994)—Smithmark Publishers Inc., New York.

Thompson, J. Eric—Maya History and Religion. (1970)—University of Oklahoma Press, Norman.

Time-Life Books--The Way of the Spirit: Nature, Myth, and Magic in Native American Life. (1997)—Time-Life Books, USA.

Wilbert, Johannes—Tobacco and Shamanism in South America. (1987)—Yale University Press, New Haven and London.

Notes

Introduction

Page

1 …releasing vile…; The Smoke of the Gods, Burns, p. 19

1 The Inquisitors, as was their way…, ibid, p. 19

1 San Salvador…; Mighty Leaf, Brooks, p. 1

1 Lands of 'vast wealth of gold…The Smoke of the Gods, Burns, p. 14

2 'fruits, wooden spares…; The Tobacco Timeline, http:/archive.tobacco.org/History/tobacco_ Histo/

2 …To look for the 'Great Khan'…The Smoke of the Gods, Burns, p. 16

4 …Carried with them…, ibid., p. 19

4 'Something to civilised man…Tobacco in Song and Story, Bain Jr., p. 9

5 The story goes…The Smoke of the Gods, Burns, pp. 24-25

5 '…men who turned gold into smoke…, ibid., p. 24

6 Jean Nicot, the French Diplomat…Tobacco in Song and Story, Bain Jr., p. 23

7 From Nicot and the Queen…, ibid., p. 23

The Oriental Connection

11 A recent discovery of 'colossal Negroid head…Before Chris Columbus, http://ryanehoward-/wordpress.com/2012/02/05/before

Page

12 The African Bantu Islamic Civilisation…, ibid.

12 *Ayurveda*, the ancient Indian…Tobacco in Ancient Indian Literature, A.R. Panchmukhi, CMDR Monograph No. 23

13 One Gentleman's Magazine…Tobacco in Song and Story, Bain Jr, p. 83

13 'tobacco is as American…Mighty Leaf, Brooks, p. 10

The Mistique Origin

15 Palaeontologists of Chiclayo…The Tobacco Timeline, http://archives.tobacco.org/History/tobacco_Histo/

16 In the Sky World…Iroquois legend, www.firstpeople.us/FP-Htn-Legends/Creation Story-Iroquois-html.

17 A legend of American Native Crow…Native American Myths and Legends, Taylor, pp. 41-43

18 The American have a long history…The Devi's Gift, https://dutchpipesmoker.wordpress.com/2013/07/09/the devil's gift.

19 A different version…Tobacco in Song and Story, Bain Jr. pp. 78-79

19 To the Algonquian Natives…The Way of the Spirit, Time-Life Books, p. 135

19 In Pigla' Mythology…Tobacco and Shamanism in South America, Wilbert, p. 151

19 Mundruchu…, ibid., 151

20 in olden Days there lived a man…Native American Folktale, www.shortstories.co.in./tobacco--fairy--blue hills

23 Long, long ago there was a Raja…When the World was Young, Elwin, pp. 32-33

24 Santal Tribesmen…Folklore of the Santal Parganas, www.urbanMyths.ca/Myths/the-origin-of-Tobacco.html.

25 There is a long standing custom among Khasis…Folktales from the Khasis, Raffy(Mrs), Ch. xiv

Page

30 The most fascinating story...Tobacco in Story and Song, Bain Jr., pp. 24-25

31 God wanted to create world...Devil's Gift, http://dutchpipesmoker.wordpress.com/2031/07/09/the-devil's gift

The Portable Altar

34 An Oglala Lakota hamlet...Walking in the Sacred Manner, Pierre & Soldier, pp. 181-182

35 'The pipe served as a portable altar...The Way of the Spirit, Time-Life Books, pp. 136-137

35 '...most ingenious...' The Smoke of the Gods, Burns, p. 3

35 Bowl of ceremonial pipes...The Way of the Spirit, Time-Life Books, pp. 136-137

35 Many, many year ago the Lakota people..., ibid., pp. 130-132 & Masterpieces of American Indian Literature, Regier, pp. 451-454

37 a man always carried a pipe...The Way of the Spirit, Time-Life Books, p. 135

37 People would blow...The smoke of the Gods, Burns, p. 3

38 Each ethnic group had...California Indians, Heizer & Whipple, pp. 22-23

39 A typical example of...Native American Myths and Legends, Taylor, pp. 112-113 & Peabody & Essex Museum, Salem, Ref. E 10

40 'Perhaps some wise man...Mighty Leaf, Brooks, p. 20

40 'tobacco smoking among Mongol..., ibid., p. 7

40 The Greco-Roman materia medica..., ibid., p. 8

41 ...the priest (or 'an impersonation...) Maya History and Religion, Thompson, pp. 106-107

42 '...a pipe in the mouth of a priest...The Smoke of the Gods, Burns, p. 11

Page

42 Popal Vuh, the K'iche' (or Quiche) Maya sacred book...
    Maya History and Religion, Thompson, p. 108

42 '...bring the firefly..., ibid., p. 108

42 'Spanish word cigarrra...Mighty Leaf, Brooks, p. 27

The Vision Quest

44 An Oglala Sioux man picked up...The Way of the Spirit,
    Time-Life Books, pp. 86-87

46 The natives of the erstwhile 'Turtle Island'...The Land Looks
    After Us, Martin, pp. 39-40

47 Wapiye' Win, the Lakota holy medicine woman...Walking
    in the Sacred Manner, Pierre & Soldier, pp. 29-31

48 '...imbibed   at   times...Maya   History   and   Religion,
    Thompson, p. 122

48 The Chorti Mayan medicine men..., ibid., p. 119

49 The efficacy of tobacco as a divine remedy...Tobacco and
    Shamanism in South America, Wilbert, pp. 189-192

50 'were despatched...Maya History and Religion, Thompson,
    p. 121

50 The Aztecs worshipped Huitzilopochtli..., ibid., pp. 113-
    114

50 Our simplistic old wold ancestors believed...Tobacco,
    Gately, p. 6

51 The term Shaman...Standard Dictionary of Folklore,
    Mythology and Legend, vol. II, Leach, p. 1003; & https://
    en.Wikipedia.org/wiki/shamanism

The Brown Gold

55 The river Yeokanta...The River Where America Began,
    Deans, p. 3

56 '...divided the ownership...Tobacco, Gately, p. 25

56 'The world we know today...The Smoke of the Gods, Burns,
    p. 19

Page

56 '…abluewaternavy…TheRiverWhereAmericaBegan,Deans,
    p. 35
56 'Spain possessed…, ibid., p. 35-36
56 '…sun never set…, ibid. p. 36
57 '…a returned mariner…Mighty Leaf, Brooks, p. 32
57 Tobacco was introduced…, ibid., p. 47
57 '…in the gardens…, ibid., p. 47
58 '…to produce a leaf…, ibid. p. 48
58 '…were not only friendly…Tobacco, Gately
59 '…from fishermen, pirates…The River Where America
    Began, Deans, p. 36
59 '…England's participation…, ibid., p. 38
59 …pointing out to the legend…, ibid., p. 39
60 '…pilfering and thieving…, ibid., p. 41
60 '…enriching the kingdom…, ibid., p. 41
60 'she was the bastard child…, ibid., p. 39
62 'a mug of ale…Tobacco, Gately, p. 51
63 The Virginia Company has chosen seven names…The River
    Where America Began, Deans, p. 52
63 '…once ensconced…, ibid. p. 53
64 '…in May 1609 the Virginia Company…, ibid., p. 90
65 'Expecting a cheerful…, ibid., p. 96
65 '…made pitch and tar…, Ibid. p. 97
66 The home bound…, ibid., p. 97
66 '…to include all lands…, ibid., pp. 97-98
66 '…while other colonists…Tobacco, Gately, p. 71
67 '…he persuaded a friend…The Smoke of the Gods, Burns,
    p. 61
68 By 1627 the shipment…Tobacco, Gately, p. 72 & Mighty
    Leaf, Brooks, p. 55
70 'The Dutch traders…Tobacco, Gately, p. 73
70 By about the middle of the eighteenth century…The Smoke
    of the Gods, Burns, p. 87
70 If there had been no slaves…, ibid., p. 87

The Globalisation

Page

83 Close on the heels of…, ibid., pp. 88-89

84 'slender form of cigar'…, ibid., 90

85 In the south-eastern fringe of the globe…www.tobaccoin Australia,org.au/8-2-history-of-tobacco-use-among-aboriginals

87 Interestingly, a chemical analysis…Evidence of tobacco in ancient Egypt, www.science. frontiers.com/sfo95a02.htm

87 After the 'reintroduction'…Smoking, Culture and Economy in the Middle East, Shechter, p.18

87 Initially they were using…, ibid. p. 18

88 Originating in the Malabar Coast…Hookah History, en.wikipedia.org/wiki/Hookah

89 The water container of the bowl…, ibid., & Smoking, Culture and Economy of the Middle East, Shechter, p. 19

89 …though hookah was of Indian origin…en.wikipedia.org/wiki/Hookah

89 The water container…The Smoking, Culture and Economy in the Middle East, Shechter, p. 19

89 By 1630s…, ibid., pp. 24-25

90 …popularly known as latakia…, ibid., p. 25

The Fad

91 '…to find a freedom…The Smoke of the Gods, Burns, p. 115

92 '…a select party of…, ibid., p. 116

92 '…yellow streams…, ibid., pp. 116-117

92 'Washington may be called…, ibid., pp. 117-118

93 …the most sickening habit…, ibid., p. 118

93 …tabagophile…Tobacco: A Cultural History of How an Exotic Plant Seduced Civilization?, Gately, p. 174

93 …Americans needed…The Smoke of the Gods, Burns, pp. 113-114

93 The chewing tobacco…, ibid., p. 115

Page

112 …a 'blustering renaissance'…, ibid., p. 203

113 '…a cigar held in hand and nursed with care…Tobacco, Gately, p. 343

116 '…in a piece of reed…The Smoke of the Gods, Burns, p. 128

116 papelito or cigarillo…, ibid., p. 130

116 '…stark naked to the waist…Tobacco, Gately, p. 179

117 '…bastardly offspring of the cigar'…Mighty Leaf, Brooks, p. 230

118 '…for its novelty…, ibid., p. 234

118 '…cigarettes seemed so tailor-made…The Smoke of the Gods, Burns, p. 131

118 '…exactly what a soldier needed…, ibid., p. 131

119 'A tobacco that could be inhaled…Tobacco, Gately, p. 184

121 James Albert Bonsak…The Smoke of the Gods, Burns, p. 134

124 To the soldier 'cigarettes were more than…, ibid., p. 20

125 The tobacco products were the promoted…Handbook of North American Indians, vol. iv, pp. 598-599

126 '…busts of prima donnas…The Mighty Leaf, Brooks, p. 264

127 '…advertising became more insistent…, ibid., p. 267

128 'Has smoking any more to do with woman's…Tobacco, Gately, p. 244

128 Edward Bernays…'He hired a group of women…The Future, Al Gore, pp. 157-158

130 'lip eroticism'…Tobacco, Gately, p. 229

130 '…effectively knocked out…, ibid., p. 246

130 'as natural as eating or kissing'…, ibid., p. 246

130 '…it now acted as the international…, ibid., p. 249

130 'a glance at the statistics proves…, ibid., p. 251

131 'most democratic commodity…, ibid., p. 252

The Fate

Page

132 The essential oil…Mighty Leaf, Brooks, p. 281

132 'agent of murder'…, ibid., p. 282

132 First warning about the health hazard…Tobacco in Ancient Indian Literature, A.R. Panchmukhi, CMDR Monograph No. 23

133 The first European to react…The Smoke of the Gods, Burns, p. 3i8

133 Pope Sixtus ordained…, ibid., p. 40

134 The latent feeling…; ibid., p. 45

136 In Russia…, ibid., 41; Tobacco, Gately, p. 85

136 'Was ever the destruction of body…The Smoke of the Gods, Burns, p. 42

136 'deemed smoking…Smoking, Culture and Economy in the Middle East, Shechter, p.16

136 …own grandson behaved…The Smoke of the Gods, Burns, p. 42

137 'an unfortunate Turk…, ibid., 41

137 'He would wander through Constantinople…, ibid., 41 & Tobacco, Gately, p. 86

137 In India…Emperor Jahangir…The Smoke of the Gods, Burns, p. 42 & Mighty leaf, Brooks, p. 77

138 'Economic and fiscal importance'…The monarchs and despots…Mighty Leaf, Brooks, pp. 80, 82

138 'The brown leaves of tobacco…, ibid., p. 108

138 All the anti-tobacco laws '…Seemed to require the expanded use…The Smoke of the Gods, Burns, p. 102

139 Benjamin Rush…, ibid., p. 98; Mighty Leaf Brooks, p. 219

141 'Tobacco was in the air…The Smoke of the Gods, Burns, p. 144

148 'cigarettes had enjoyed…Tobacco, Gately, p. 265

148 'The soldiers who survived one enemy…The Smoke of the Gods, Burns, p. 208

Page

150 Humphrey Bogart…Tobacco, Gately, p. 286

155 '…three hundred young people…The Smoke of the Gods, Burns, pp. 233-234

155 A very recent survey, conducted by the New York…Times of India, 08.07.2014

The Future

157 Some corporate houses…Kashmir Reader, Srinagar, 19-05-2015

157 Researchers from the Universities…Brighter Kashmir, Srinagar, 12-05-2015

158 Psychologists and tobacco-addiction specialists…Asian Age, New Delhi, 20-05-2015

158 An Israeli scientist…Times of India, Calcutta, 12-06-2010

158 Charles Kingsley…Tobacco, Gately, p. 197

159 Sir Compton Mackenzie…, ibid., p. 283

159 Albert Einstein…, ibid., p. 220

Epilogue

161 A news item…Tobacco in Song and Story, Bain Jr., p. 54

161 Harvard Medical researchers…Tobacco, Gately, p. 357

162 A survey jointly undertaken…Times of India, Calcutta, 30-03-2013

162 A British official survey…Tobacco, Gately, pp. 353-354

162 Louis-Napoleon III…, ibid., p. 181

162 Conversation between General Montgomery…, ibid., p. 257

163 The president of the anti-cigarette League…, ibid., p. 230

163 Larry White…, ibid., p. 354

Index